Open
Management

Open
Management

by Vincent W. Kafka
and John H. Schaefer

PETER H. WYDEN/PUBLISHER

New York

Open Management

LIBRARY OF CONGRESS CATALOG CARD NUMBER: 74-22947

ISBN: 0-88326-081-6

MANUFACTURED IN THE UNITED STATES OF AMERICA

This book
is dedicated
with love

to
Betty

and

to
Diane

Contents

Open
Management

1. WHAT OPEN MANAGEMENT IS

You have chosen a meaningful book. Everyone who comes into contact with people in the business world will find it useful and refreshing, though perhaps strange on first acquaintance.

Open Management is a brand-new concept for dealing with people at work. It is quite literally practical: It shows managers and employees new ways to practice in order to get more done and feel more worthwhile when working with others.

Why should people really be all that concerned about other people in an organization? Because whenever a problem emerges that involves the four essential elements of organizations—people, machines, materials, and money—the problem usually stems from (and can be resolved by) the people concerned. Obviously, if people—managers and employees—are the most important element in any organization, and if problems are resolved by people, then time spent learning why people do the things they do and say the things they say is time that could hardly be better spent.

So welcome to the Open Management Club, where there are no hidden motivations, no wily manipulations, no factions or sides, and, most important, no secrets that cover up human relationships in the work environment; only better understanding, greater productivity, enhanced motivation, and more satisfaction at every level, from janitor to president. Everybody understands the other person better. Everybody benefits. Nobody loses.

Much has been written about the manager's role and the development of management personnel. Attempts have also been made to see the work environment from the employee's point of view. Open Management is a unique technique for exploring and appreciating the viewpoints of *all* people in the work environment, simultaneously and in such a complementary way that each person will grow to understand the viewpoint of the others. The techniques developed in this book will do much to help any manager *and* any employee to develop a better understanding of the environment in which they work and to develop personal job satisfaction. It explores both sides of the fence at once and gives equal emphasis to both.

Open Management is really about the satisfaction

of individual human needs. When these are satisfied on the job, a person's effectiveness is greatly increased. Since this is equally true of managers and employees, Open Management addresses itself to both groups, and managers can usefully recommend this book to employees.

To learn about people, one may build upon the great discoveries of the past, but what has been missing is a practical way to relate these theories to the work experience. Open Management is that way.

One difficulty with personal experiences is that their impact can be understood fully only by those who participated in them. Yet knowledge of certain experiences can tell a lot about a person. When a manager speaks of the Great Depression of the 1930s, he is trying to share a personal experience. If his audience is made up of young people who were not born until after the depression, they probably do not appreciate or even understand what the manager is saying; they are not able to feel the impact or share the depression experiences—but through the Open Management System (OMS) these same people could be able to understand more about the person who is describing them.

A young employee, in talking to his manager about his need for "interesting" and "challenging" work, may show utter disregard for the many fringe benefits, such as job security and pension rights, which the older man holds in high regard. Through Open Management, the manager becomes able to understand more about the employee's viewpoint.

People at work need job identity. One recent study

of work environments found that approximately 75 percent of workers under thirty years of age did *not* derive a great deal of satisfaction from the work they were doing. This percentage dropped only slightly for older people; it remained above 50 percent even for those at retirement age.

These staggering statistics show clearly that many people obtain very little personal job satisfaction from their work. Yet, when work has no meaning, life has no meaning. So employees today ask such questions as "Why am I doing this work?" If such questions cannot be answered satisfactorily, managers and employees are in great difficulty indeed.

Open Management shows how to provide individual satisfaction by creating an environment in which open understanding can grow between people on the job. It helps to create a positive atmosphere; not only are individual human needs satisfied, but the entire organization gains.

Much has been written about motivating others. Actually, motivation stems from actions that satisfy individual human needs. It is individual and internal. Actions come from within a person when the environment permits them to occur. In reality, everyone in an organization motivates himself. Only when he does so can he make a contribution to the overall environment.

When a person's individual human needs are satisfied, he feels like a winner. When a person helps another person to satisfy *his* human needs, he too feels like a winner. The Open Management System provides a means to create a win-win situation between any two people in the business environment.

Open Management recognizes that every person is

endowed with specific talents and potential. All too often, an individual manager or employee works at a very small portion of this potential, even though he may be very busy most of the time. If a plane can carry one hundred passengers but travels between Points A and B with only forty passengers, it is working at 40 percent of its potential, shuttling busily back and forth, using fuel and tying up a crew that can service one hundred.

Similarly, people on the job can be busy—but working at only a fraction of their potential. Application of Open Management principles helps to create the environment for all people to have the opportunity of working closer to their potential.

Obviously, when a person works a full day in a positive environment, his work is meaningful and has positive impact; in a negative environment, he may be just as busy, but his motivation is mostly to *look* busy. Total output is necessarily below potential; the impact is negative, and especially there is no self-fulfillment.

Charlie Pickett was an office supervisor who complained regularly about the low output of his employees. When asked about this, Charlie replied, "I can't understand it. Every time I check up on them, everyone is busy." Yet morale in Charlie's section was considerably lower than in other sections.

When confronted with this situation, Charlie decided that what was needed was closer supervision of what each employee was doing. Charlie felt that close follow-up would increase output, and that people would feel better knowing he was more aware of their performance.

In order to do this, Charlie installed three large

convex mirrors so that he could observe everyone in the section without ever leaving his desk. Charlie reported this new arrangement to his boss, and commented, "With this new setup, I'll really be able to tell who is goofing off, and will be able to take the appropriate action."

During the first two weeks after the mirrors were installed, Charlie noted that everyone appeared to be busy—but, astonishingly, the productivity of his section had fallen to a new low. Charlie wondered what to do next.

Helen Larson, the head teller in a bank, had received a number of complaints about one of her tellers. The complaints indicated that this teller tended to be rude to customers, especially during busy periods. In addition, Helen had noted that this teller often was late for work.

Helen decided to have lunch with this girl and explore the situation in some detail. As a result of this special attention, Helen noted that she received fewer complaints about rudeness, and that during the following week the teller was more punctual. Helen was very pleased with this improvement, but wondered what it was that had brought it about. She thought, "It might have been my talk with her, but why would such a little thing have made such a big difference?"

Arthur Lynch, a design draftsman, overheard one of his fellow draftsmen complaining about the way he was being treated. When Arthur inquired what was wrong, the man replied, "Over the weekend my drafting table was moved. I don't have the work space I had before. I notice you weren't moved at all."

Arthur, a perceptive employee, understood that his fellow employee was upset over not having been consulted about the relocation of his work table, as well as the actual loss of space. Therefore, he suggested that they both move their work tables to more effectively utilize the space available. This suggestion was well received by the other employee, and both were able to continue working. Arthur felt pleased, but wondered how a "little thing" like work space could be so upsetting.

Ralph Bingham was a field engineer working on a large mining construction project. Ralph observed that a minor change in the design of the loading conveyor would make it more easily adjustable in the field. On his next visit to the project, Ralph told his boss that he should recommend making this change at once, to avoid future expense and delays in conveyor installations. Ralph's boss replied emphatically, "I've worked with this conveyor system for twelve years, and I know every inch of it. If there are going to be any changes made, I'll let you know how to design them."

Ralph walked away totally disgusted, wondering how he could get along with his boss in the future.

Situations like these happen every day in every work environment. Usually, whether the outcome is favorable or unfavorable, there is little understanding of why something worked or failed. For years managers and employees have searched for practical solutions to motivational problems on the job. Open Management's unique approach benefits both managers and employees. If one person in the work environment can see the other person's point of view, he not only understands the problem better but has a better chance of developing a solution.

Open Management is based on open-mindedness. It provides the tools for every manager and every employee to increase personal satisfaction on the job. The quality of work in America is a subject of growing concern to managers as well as employees. Open Management provides answers to the questions of how the quality of work can be improved to everyone's satisfaction.

2. THE THREE PRINCIPLES OF OPEN MANAGEMENT

N OPEN Management, well-established principles are combined into a system that can be used by any manager or any employee on any job. A synergistic relationship between these basic principles is developed, so that the results are greater than the individual application of each separate principle. This chapter is an overview of these various princples. Each will be discussed in detail in subsequent chapters.

The first of these principles is: *See a situation from the other person's point of view.*

Alice Hayward was secretary to Hoyt Melville, Director of Environmental Affairs in the Bellville regional office. Alice took every opportunity to talk to people working in the office. Other employees stopped by regularly to see her and discuss subjects unconnected with work. Alice also spent a great deal of time talking on the phone with people in other offices.

Hoyt had been growing more and more concerned about Alice's excessive talkativeness. But he didn't seem to know what to do, until he looked at the problem from Alice's point of view. Putting himself in Alice's place, he began to see that Alice's chattiness was a part of her work style and her gregarious nature. Viewing the situation solely from his own point of view, Hoyt might have tried to stop Alice's excessive talking. But in that kind of office this would have been virtually impossible without stifling Alice's natural ability to get along with people.

By seeing the situation from Alice's point of view, Hoyt realized the importance to his department of having someone with Alice's qualities. Therefore, Hoyt suggested to Alice positive ways to talk—discussing some of the department's activities with other people in the company; this liaison program would give other people in the company a better understanding of his own department's objectives. Hoyt thereby created a motivational environment so Alice could make positive contributions in her work—from her own point of view—which ultimately benefited everyone.

The principle is applicable to any person-to-person relationship. Consider the following.

Don Schmidt, a new-accounts clerk, was very conscientious in his job. His boss, Bob Grover, was responsible for resolving any problems regarding new customer accounts locally. Bob frequently spent several hours a day out of the office. This was frustrating to Don, who often had to wait for Bob to return in order to have new-account procedures approved.

By applying the OMS principle of seeing a situation from another person's point of view, Don tried to see Bob's job from Bob's point of view.

In doing so, Don began to realize that Bob's time spent away from the office was an important part of his job, and essential for developing new customers. On one occasion, when Don was discussing the opening of a new account with a customer, the customer mentioned how much she was impressed by Bob's efforts to be helpful in their community organization. She indicated that this was one of the reasons for her opening an account with his company.

Don then thought to himself, "I guess I was right about the importance of Bob's customer calls. It really pays off to have Bob spend so much of his time out of the office."

These two cases show how managers and employees both benefit from attempts to understand a situation from the other person's viewpoint. This has even greater impact when used in conjunction with the second principle of Open Management: *Identify (and build on) an individual's strengths, rather than concentrating on how to improve weaknesses.* Be aware of what a person does uncommonly well, rather than focusing on what that person does not do well.

Clyde Morrissey was interviewing candidates for a first-line supervisor's job. The outstanding candidate for the job was Sandra Farnsworth, who was highly recommended and well qualified because of her education and work experience. But Clyde concentrated on trying to find out where each candidate was weak. His philosophy was that this would tell him where to concentrate his attention after a person was hired.

In the interview with Sandra, Clyde put so much emphasis on her weaknesses that he lost sight of her great strengths—and how they overshadowed her weaknesses. Since her weaknesses were in areas that Clyde did not feel he could improve substantially, he did not select her for the supervisor's job. In fact, Sandra was the best candidate for this job, and would have performed exceedingly well. Clyde's failure to identify Sandra's strengths caused him to lose a potentially outstanding employee.

Another example of the importance of identifying strengths rather than weaknesses is Ray Zeitlow, an inspector in the Quality Control Group. His boss, Burl Mumford, the chief inspector of the group, had been with Quality Control for twenty-eight years, and believed that the company should not tolerate any deviation from the standards that had been developed. On several occasions Burl had run head-on into conflicts with other department heads regarding product quality. This conscientious regard for high quality was one of Burl's outstanding strengths.

Because Ray recognized this strength in his boss, he maintained a very high level of quality in his work, and could take pride in it. By recognizing Burl's strength, Ray created a pleasant work environment for himself and Burl. Consequently, Ray was able to maintain a good relationship with Burl—something that many others could not do, because they were unable to identify Burl's strength. Result: Both Ray's productivity and the quality of his work remained high.

These two cases show that identification of strengths is essential to a positive motivational environment. But for Open Management to be used most effectively, it is necessary to incorporate a third principle: *Understand and satisfy an individual's human needs.*

The human needs discussed here are psychological human needs of every person. These needs are described in detail in Chapter 5, but the following examples will illustrate the application of this principle.

Bill Murphy, a production manager, had a problem with one of his clerks, Jim Tessorïo, whose production had fallen off. Bill knew that Jim had good potential and could do much better, and he arranged to get Jim a hefty raise. Jim appeared to be very pleased. For a couple of weeks, there was some increase in Jim's productivity. Then, much to Bill's surprise, Jim's productivity sagged back to where it was before he got the raise.

The reason: The raise Bill got for Jim apparently did not satisfy one of Jim's psychological human needs, and Bill never bothered to find out what that need was.

Another example concerns Agnes Thompson, a saleswoman in a local department store, who worked for Beverly Morgan, the department's buyer. Agnes realized that Beverly had a strong need for recognition. Accordingly, Agnes regularly acknowledged in a positive way that Beverly's abilities contributed to the department's success. As a result, Agnes created a pleasant environment in which she and Beverly were able to work together effectively.

Many times in a manager-employee relationship

people tend to think of one side as winning and the other as losing. For example, when Clyde Morrissey did not hire Sandra Farnsworth, he probably thought of himself as a winner as he chose someone else. Clyde also saw Sandra as losing (the job). Sandra may also have seen herself as losing and someone else as winning. This is typical of person-to-person relationships in business everywhere. People are conditioned to think in terms of winning and losing.

But in this case both Clyde and Sandra were losers: Clyde lost an outstanding candidate; Sandra lost this opportunity for a good job.

By applying the principles of the Open Management System, both Clyde and Sandra could have been winners. If Clyde had recognized Sandra's strengths, he would have won an outstanding employee, and she would have won the job.

In the situation of Agnes Thompson and Beverly Morgan, Agnes, the perceptive employee, created a situation that satisfied Beverly's need for recognition. At the same time, she created a better work environment for herself—because her boss's human needs were satisfied.

Who was the loser in this situation? No one. Both Agnes and Beverly were winners, because Beverly's need for recognition was satisfied and Agnes was able to find satisfaction in her work. But more than these two people were involved in this win-win relationship; also involved were other employees and managers and, perhaps most important to this situation, customers—and they all benefited.

We all know the good feeling that comes with being a winner. In the Open Management System, the opportunities for creating win-win situations is greatly increased.

In summary, the three basic principles of the Open Management System are:

1. *See a situation from the other person's point of view.*

2. *Identify and build on an individual's strengths, rather than concentrating on how to improve weaknesses.*

3. *Understand and satisfy the individual's human needs.*

These three basic principles together provide an approach to working effectively with other people. Each may be used individually, but it is their synergistic *combination* that really gets results.

Since most of a manager's time is spent working with people, his effectiveness is related to how effectively he utilizes available time. OMS will help him to make the most effectively use of his time.

True, the more people one supervises, the more critical becomes the time spent with each person. The OMS concepts work because they help a manager to make the best use of the time he has available for each person. It is like tasting a fresh apple pie. Eating one slice is usually sufficient to determine if you like the pie. It is not necessary to eat the whole pie. So it is in working with people. It is not necessary to know everything about a person in order to identify and understand human needs. Managers and employees have always spent time seeing and hearing other people's actions. OMS does not ask for any more time. Instead, it helps to show managers and employees a better use of their time by making them more aware of the needs being represented by their words and actions.

OMS helps managers and employees to work more effectively with one another. How can one spend time better? All too often both managers and employees waste considerable time with ineffective efforts. OMS helps to eliminate all that wasted effort by zeroing in directly on the heart of the matter—the satisfying of individual human needs.

An intellectual study of management is no more effective than an intellectual study of a sport. To achieve proficiency, it is necessary to practice constantly. OMS encourages people to practice the right thing. As one develops familiarity with the OMS approach, the amount of time required to identify and understand individual human needs lessens. Thus practice makes practical the application of the OMS system in any situation.

3. SEEING A SITUATION FROM THE OTHER PERSON'S POINT OF VIEW

HERE, AND wherever practical in subsequent chapters, we will divide our discussion into three parts. First we will explore the theoretical aspects of the principle; then the relationship of the theory to the practical aspects of the *manager*'s job; and then to the practical aspects of the *employee*'s job.

Everybody can think of many benefits that can result from seeing another person's point of view:

You can gain a better understanding of the person who is extremely cautious about money by trying to recognize the many possible reasons for his caution. Or take the person who drives a car with excessive care; you get insight into his behavior if you can identify some of his motivations.

"Empathy" is the term often used to describe seeing a situation from the other person's point of view. We all try to empathize from time to time, but often we remain unable to see the other person's viewpoint. This failure usually causes people to stop trying to empathize. But in OMS we suggest that only a little bit of understanding—or empathy—can have very positive results. Why? Because it is the first step in creating the person-to-person relationships essential for a good work environment. Total understanding of another person's viewpoint is not necessary; it is quite sufficient to understand only a small part. From this beginning it is possible to effect significant changes.

This might be likened to water heated to 211 degrees Fahrenheit, at which point it is merely hot water. When heated to 212 degrees, the water boils, and some of it becomes steam, which has the potential to do great work. The difference is 1 degree, but that degree has enormous consequences.

Here's an analogy relating to this principle: In a swim meet the winner often finishes less than a second ahead of the runner-up; sometimes the time differential can be gauged only by sophisticated electronic timing devices. But it is this small difference in time which determines the champion.

So, too, with empathy: A little bit can make a crucial difference for any manager or employee. For the manager, empathy can be the means for creating a meaningful motivational environment. For the employee, empathy leads to an understanding of why the boss does the things he does.

A person's viewpoint is the product of the many different factors which have influenced his experience: Heredity, environment, education, health, religion, family, social influences, money, occupation, political affiliations all contribute to a point of view.

We can illustrate (Figure 1) with a circle encompassing all the many elements that determine a particular viewpoint.

Figure 1

As we can see, these elements are overlapping and blended together. The perceptive person, while seeing another as a whole, will keep in mind that the other person's viewpoint is really made up of many overlapping elements, and, like the bits and pieces in a kaleidoscope, a slight change in the arrangement can have a noticeable impact on the person's total viewpoint.

Each person's viewpoint is unique. Whenever two people meet and communicate, two separate viewpoints are involved. Each sees the other's viewpoint as being separate—and different—from his own.

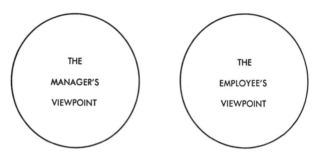

Figure 2

The two circles in Figure 2 represent the separate viewpoints of two persons. But an awareness of the other person's viewpoint can result in an area of understanding between those two people (Figure 3).

Area of Understanding

Figure 3

As we can see, the area of understanding is not a large one, but—as in the case of the hot water, or the swim meet—a small change can make a significant difference. Ordinarily, the larger the area of understanding, the better the relationship between two persons.

But what factors contribute to an increase in the

area of understanding? If we go back to Figure 2, for example, what forces will tend to move them further apart?

We will call any forces that move the two viewpoints closer together "convergent forces," and any that move them away from each other "divergent forces" (Figure 4).

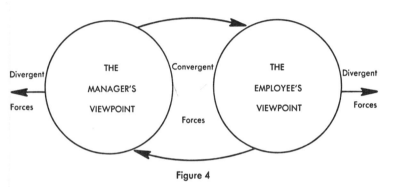

Figure 4

Examples of convergent forces would include such things as:

1. A desire on the part of one person to understand the other. The stronger the desire and the more positive the person's attitude, the better the chance for achieving an area of understanding.

2. Having clearly defined goals which are compatible with the goals of the other person.

3. Having interests similar to those of the other person.

4. Being willing to listen to the other person.

5. Being a good observer of the other person.

6. Being a good communicator.

7. Being sincerely interested in the other person.

Examples of divergent forces would include such things as:

1. Indifference to the other person's point of view.
2. Vague or general goals which are hard to define.
3. Interests dissimilar from those of the other person.
4. Talking about oneself rather than listening to the other person.
5. Ignoring what we observe in the other person.
6. Inability to communicate.
7. Not caring about the other person.

In the Open Management System, the emphasis is on convergent forces: the ones that make it easier to see the other person's point of view and create an area of understanding as large as possible.

An important point: It isn't necessary to agree with another person in order to develop an area of understanding. Two people may disagree, yet each can understand why the other acts as he does—and benefit thereby.

Developing an area of understanding is an important first step in creating an environment in which both manager and employee achieve job satisfaction.

THE MANAGER'S VIEWPOINT

Edward Fletcher, a research analyst, often saw his boss, John Kelley, coming in late to work. Ed frequently told his co-workers how angry it made him that managers could come to work any time they wanted to, while others had to adhere to a rigid time schedule. On several occasions he took up the time of other people in the office to complain about this. Things came to a head when Ed noticed that a memo was posted on a bulletin board that emphasized that *all* employees were required to be at work in their designated area at the specified time.

The new ruling was issued by Paul Carruthers, the general manager, who had noted that some employees were regularly late for work and that in general most employees were very slow in getting started.

The very next day, for the fourth time that month, John Kelley was an hour late. When Ed saw him come in, he immediately got into a huddle with three other employees and told them how "burned up" he was that some people had to follow rules while others didn't. The others, infected by Ed's anger, agreed, and wondered why such unfair practices should exist in what they otherwise regarded as a good company.

Productivity began to drop off noticeably as a result of this dissatisfaction among employees in the Research Department. Naturally, John quickly became aware of this and, a perceptive manager, began to search for a reason. When he talked to his people, it soon became apparent that from their point of view his lateness was a direct violation of the company's standard practice. John knew that Ed was an influential member of the group. He also knew that Ed was a punctual person, with a reputation for always being on time. Realizing how his own tardiness was affecting Ed and the others, John decided to meet with Ed informally.

At this meeting, John explained that he regularly attended a number of breakfast conferences held by professional organizations to which he belonged. He emphasized their importance: By going, John kept himself informed of current happenings in his field, and was able to keep his company abreast of changing situations.

These breakfast meetings were important to all concerned. So, John explained to Ed, even though he was not present in the office, he was not late—in fact, he was "at work" long before many of the others. Ed seemed very interested in what John was saying. And so John, the perceptive manager, invited Ed to attend the next breakfast meeting with him.

Several weeks after John and Ed talked, John noted an improvement in the morale of his group; productivity was on the rise again, and Ed had come up with several innovative ideas—something he had not done for months.

In reflecting on this, John realized that his own lateness must have looked as if he were flouting the rules. Had he not recognized how things appeared from the employees' point of view, the situation probably would have worsened or, at best, continued as a source of frustration and dissatisfaction.

John could have done one of several things: He might have taken disciplinary action; he could have ignored the situation. Instead, in applying the first principle of OMS, he tried to see the problem from the employees' point of view, and in understanding their dissatisfaction take the right action to resolve it.

Here's another, less happy example of how the manager's viewpoint can affect employees: Ralph Peabody was the manager of Computer Operations for a large company. Harvey Riggs was one of Ralph's key supervisors. Harvey's job required that he be away from his office for several hours each day. Sometimes he had to be away for two or three days at a time. Occasionally he returned to the office quite late in the day—sometimes even after closing time. Often, on returning late, he found messages from Ralph saying, "Please see me."

Whenever he received one of these messages, Harvey became very concerned. Harvey was a conscientious supervisor, and liked to be prepared to answer any questions Ralph might have had. But since Ralph's messages never said why he wanted to see Harvey, Harvey could only worry.

On one such occasion, Harvey returned to the office on Friday evening after a three-day business trip. He stopped in to pick up his mail and found one of Ralph's "Please see me" messages. Because there were several important matters pending, but Harvey felt he shouldn't trouble Ralph at home, Harvey spent the entire weekend worrying.

If Ralph had been aware of the impact these messages had on Harvey, he might have resolved the situation. But Ralph made no effort to see the situation from Harvey's point of view; he saw it only from his own. As the manager of Computer Operations, Ralph felt justified in requesting meetings with his subordinates whenever the situation required them. From Ralph's point of view, "Please see me" simply meant "I would like to have a meeting with you when you return." From Harvey's point of view, "Please see me" could mean anything from "You're doing a great job" to "Where is the report on the Brisbane account?" It was the uncertainty that troubled him. If Ralph had understood how these three simple words "Please see me" affected another person's point of view, he might have changed.

Unfortunately, many managers like Ralph never realize how the little, seemingly unimportant things they do and say appear to the employee. If they would only look at the situation from the other person's point of view, they would realize that these "little" things can be *very* important and can have significant positive or negative results.

THE EMPLOYEE'S VIEWPOINT

Mark Flint was a design engineer who worked for Harry Chan, manager of the Design Engineering Section. Mark was an extremely competent young engineer who had earned his Master's Degree in engineering at night school and made every effort to stay abreast in his field. He had even taken an after-hours assignment at the local community college: One evening a week he taught design engineering at the school. Mark's class was popular with the students, and he was regarded as an excellent teacher.

Mark valued his extra work as a good way to keep up with current engineering practices. Many of the younger draftsmen in the company had taken Mark's course, and they too had found it worthwhile. All this made Mark a valuable employee, both to his company and to Harry Chan.

One morning, Harry saw Mark working at his desk and asked what he was doing. Mark replied, "I'm getting my lessons organized for the evening classes I'm teaching." Harry, seeing the situation from his own point of view, said, "Mark, so long as you're working for me, I want you to spend all your time on company projects, not your own."

Until then Mark had felt that by teaching the course, by keeping up with the latest engineering practices, and by helping other employees he was doing a good job for his company. From Mark's point of view, using company time for these related activities made sense. Because of them, he was able to resolve difficult design problems more quickly. And his teaching the other draftsmen made *them* more valuable to the company. Mark had felt justified in spending a few hours of company time preparing for his classes.

As he thought about what Harry had said, Mark realized that not everyone shared his viewpoint—to put it mildly. Therefore, he decided to talk things over with Harry.

Harry had been the section manager for two years. He was also a competent engineer, and very conscientious about his work. He was well-organized, and took great pride in the quality of the work produced by his section.

In the meeting between Mark and Harry, Mark, a perceptive employee, kept Harry's viewpoint in mind. He explained to Harry that what he was doing on company time was directly related to the work of the section and beneficial to the section's productivity and reputation for innovative design work. As a result of Mark's approach, an area of understanding between Mark and Harry began to emerge.

As a perceptive manager, Harry saw how Mark's contribution really did benefit the entire section. Mark and Harry together explored the possibility of Mark's conducting some in-company training programs.

Mark, in perceiving Harry's point of view—and in creating an environment in which Harry could understand Mark's point of view—created a win-win situation. Mark was able to continue his teaching both on and off the job and stay current in his field while helping others. Harry was able to maintain a high level of productivity and enhance the reputation of his section for quality performance. And, since both Mark and Harry gained, so did the company. All were winners.

OMS concentrates on the person, not the job. By concentrating on the person, not only does the job get done, but the person gets satisfaction while doing it.

Another example of the impact of the employee's viewpoint is illustrated in the following example. Tony Lorenzi was a Procedures clerk in the Westwood office. Because of a system-wide change in reporting procedures, a new Procedures Manual had to be developed. This was such a large and urgent project that the Procedures manager at headquarters, D. Franklin Mueller, asked each of the company's six regional offices to send one of their Procedures clerks to headquarters for a six-month period; after that the clerk would return to his former job. Tony Lorenzi was selected to be the Westwood representative on the project.

At first Tony was enthusiastic about this new assignment and most anxious to make a contribution. But after two months Tony's enthusiasm had diminished greatly. What had seemed to be an ideal opportunity turned out to be something quite different, from Tony's point of view. To begin with, Mr. Mueller never bothered to introduce Tony to others in the headquarters organization. Tony had been given a tiny, enclosed office with no name on the door to indicate who worked there. From Tony's point of view, he was a nonentity working among strangers on a minuscule part of the project.

Tony felt strongly about having his name on the door, and decided to mention the matter to Mr. Mueller. Mr. Mueller replied to Tony's requent with "Lorenzi, you'll be back at your regular job in Westwood in four months. It just isn't worth spending the money to do that sort of thing. After all, if we did it for you, we'd have to do it for everyone who comes in here on a rotational assignment."

Tony returned to his office thoroughly dejected. His former enthusiasm was gone, and he waited impatiently for the completion of his assignment so that he could return to Westwood. From his point of view, having his name on the door would not only have provided him some recognition but would have improved company communication.

But from D. Franklin Mueller's point of view, putting names on doors for rotational employees didn't make sense in terms of the money involved.

If Tony had been able to see the situation from Mr. Mueller's point of view, he might have been able to create an area of understanding and in so doing get his name on the door. But Tony saw the situation only from his own point of view, so no understanding was developed, and he did not get his name on the office door.

These incidents show how important it is to see a situation from the other person's point of view. The principle applies to managers as well as to employees. When points of view are shared, it is possible to develop an area of understanding—and it is only within this area of understanding that a win-win situation can occur. As we've also seen, not understanding the other person's point of view can be very damaging indeed.

Recognizing the importance of seemingly insignificant details can lead to greater areas of understanding. When both manager and employee do this, everyone wins.

4. IDENTIFYING AND BUILDING ON INDIVIDUAL STRENGTHS

EVERYONE HAS strengths. Identifying and building on them is the second principle of OMS. And, as we have said, too often managers and employees take a negative approach, looking for what is wrong with the other person rather than for what is right, seeing only the other person's weaknesses.

Our society often stresses weaknesses and what is not done well. In our lifestyle as well as our work style, we spend a lot of time trying to overcome weaknesses—time that would be better spent on developing strengths.

We never hear anyone actually say, "Forget about a person's strengths." But by implication, when someone says, "Let's correct these weaknesses," strengths are deemphasized, and are bound to weaken. We're not suggesting that weaknesses be overlooked. By all means improve them. But, more important, identify your strengths and build on them.

The world is filled with people who succeed by building on their strengths.

Take Mark Spitz, for example, who in the 1972 World Olympics won seven Gold Medals for swimming. This was a fantastic feat, and Mark is undoubtedly the greatest swimmer of his time. As a young boy Mark was already a strong and talented swimmer. It is conceivable, though, that if someone had said, "Mark, you're already a wonderful swimmer, how about developing abilities in some other sports so that you'll become an all-around athlete?" he might not have become the first person to win seven Olympic Gold Medals.

Many people feel it's necessary to be "well rounded"—to develop abilities in many different areas. While this may be a goal worth striving for, the fact is that most men and women are lopsided where talent is concerned. Finding out what particular talents a person possesses, and allowing him to *use* them, is the best way to achieve superior performance in any field.

Job satisfaction depends to a great degree on being able to exercise one's special abilities. Unfortunately, many people spend their entire lives doing whatever comes along without ever considering whether they're working in an area where they can use their talents. No wonder that for them a job is just a way to collect a paycheck.

Of course, great genius rarely goes unnoticed. But ordinary mortals are often unaware of where their special strengths lie. One way to recognize your own (and other people's) strengths is to keep track of daily job activities and rate them. To do this, make up a chart similar to the one shown in Figure 5.

STRENGTH ANALYSIS

	Dislikes									Likes
	0 1 2 3 4 5 6 7 8 9 10									
Things I Do	Minimum				Average				Maximum	

Figure 5

List each daily activity in the column on the left and make an evaluation according to how you feel about doing it. For instance, if one of the things you do is write lengthy reports, and you dislike writing them, you might give this activity a 0, 1, or 2 rating. If talking with customers on the phone is an activity you enjoy, you might rate it in the maximum area: an 8, 9, or 10.

We suggest that you keep a log of job activities for at least two weeks. At the end of this time you should have a long list of items—the longer the better. As you review your list, pay particular attention to the items with very low ratings, as well as the ones rated very high. Obviously, the high-rated activities are the things you like doing best. Can you see a pattern? Most people find that the activities they enjoy are the ones they do best, and therefore constitute areas of special strengths.

It may be that you spend only a small portion of your day working in your "strong" areas. Even so, it's likely that you are making a significant contribution during that time. Obviously, the more time you spend working in your strong areas, the happier you will be and the greater your contribution to your work group.

This method of identifying strengths can be used in several ways. It is a help in evaluating one's present job. It indicates why a particular person is happy and does well in a particular job—or, conversely, why he or she is unhappy and doing poorly. It can also be a decision-making factor in choosing whether or not to switch jobs.

Suppose you are considering a change. You might wish to use this method to analyze the new job—and be in a better position to make a sound decision.

To rate a potential new job, you would list in as much detail as possible the individual duties required by the job, and rate them in exactly the same way you rated activities on your present job. With the information from these ratings, you would be able to determine whether you would like the new job—and whether it would allow you to utilize your strengths.

The chart on the following page shows how one young man analyzed a potential new job.

Upon completing the analysis, he decided to take the job, for the following reasons:

1. There were more activities that he liked than he disliked.

2. His strength analysis for this particular job indicated that he enjoyed doing what the job requires.

STRENGTH ANALYSIS

Job Activities I Would Be Doing	0 Minimum	1	2	3	4	5 Average	6	7	8	9 Maximum	10
Contact customers											
at their business										9	
at home									8		
by phone								7			
Evening meetings							6				
Driving car										9	
Write reports				3							
Weekend duty							6				
Making technical layouts								7			
Working with other departments								7			
Out of town meetings			2								
Keeping myself informed									8		

Figure 6

One of the key considerations for any person identifying likes and dislikes for a job is the time required for each job activity. If the job evaluated in Figure 6 required that the young man spend 70 percent of his time writing reports, then he probably should not have taken the job; if he spent 70 percent of his time on an activity he disliked, he would get very little satisfaction from his work. He would also be concentrating most of his efforts in an area that was not his strength. Or he might have put off the activity as much as possible—and ended up further and further behind in his reports. By his avoiding his dislikes and the activities in which he lacked strength, the job would have suffered, and so would he.

Many people think they already know how they feel about the different aspects of their jobs. But in rating all the activities involved in a particular job, one gets a good, clear overview of the work itself, and why it does or doesn't contribute to a sense of satisfaction.

Of course, in addition to the opportunity to work in the areas of one's strengths, there are other things to consider when deciding whether to change jobs; factors such as environment, family, future opportunities, money all come into play. No attempt is being made here to suggest that any one factor is more important than any other. Rating one's strengths is simply a tool—though an important one—which can be helpful in making the right decision.

The method for identifying strengths, incidentally, will not only help you analyze your own areas of special competence; it can also help you discover hidden strengths that lie within each person in your organization.

There are other areas in which a strength analysis is helpful. Suppose you're wondering whether or not to take up golf. Before you invest heavily in equipment, you can list all the component activities in golfing. (Figure 7 on page 36 gives an approximate breakdown.)

If the likes and dislikes indicated in Figure 7 represent the way you see yourself as a golfer, should you take up golf? The answer at first would appear to be no. However, the real answer is that it depends on the *importance* of your *maximum* likes. If being outdoors with friends is very enjoyable to you, perhaps golf is a good sport choice despite the fact that you hate getting up early, etc. In other words, consider whether the maximum likes outweigh the maximum dislikes.

Of course, you could also get outdoor exercise with friends by planning volleyball, tennis, croquet, or touch football, and you could do a strength analysis on any or all of these other sports. The point is that by analyzing strengths you stand to save yourself a lot of time, energy, and, possibly, money.

STRENGTH ANALYSIS

Golfing Activities I Would Be Doing	Dislikes 0 Minimum	1	2	3	4	5 Average	6	7	8	Likes 9 Maximum	10
Hunting for lost balls	0										
Getting caught in the rain		1									
Being with friends									8		
Outdoor exercise										9	
Walking			1								
Get up early			1								
Hitting golf ball (pretending it's someone you know)				2							
						5					
Carrying golf bag		1									
or pushing cart		1									
or riding in cart				2							
Fame for making hole-in-one				2							
Relaxation on 19th hole								7			

Figure 7

In any case, it is important to know where one's strengths lie. People who like what they are doing are happier. People who work in the areas of their strengths are working closer to their potential. For these reasons, the second principle of the Open Management System is important to both managers and employees.

THE MANAGER'S VIEWPOINT

Frank Hernandez had been with Cramer Accounting Services for over ten years. Frank started working for Cramer immediately after he graduated from high school. His first job was as the office mailboy. It was the policy at Cramer to promote from within, and much emphasis was placed on personal development; night school, weekend seminars, and correspondence courses were encouraged. During his years with Cramer, Frank's supervisors urged him to continue his education in accounting, pointing out that this would help him to get ahead at Cramer.

Frank held several different clerical jobs at Cramer. All of his supervisors rated Frank very highly on his ability to get along with his fellow workers. Once, soon after Frank had been transferred to a new department, a long-standing conflict between two of the employees appeared to have settled itself. Actually, it was Frank's ability to understand and communicate with people that had resolved the feud. The department supervisor was perceptive and recognized Frank's contribution as peacemaker, and that the department was functioning more effectively because Frank had this talent. He remarked: "Frank certainly does have a knack for working with people. Our group never worked together as well in the past."

For some years Frank had been going to night school, and just last year received a degree in accounting. Shortly after receiving his degree, Frank was promoted to the job of Specialist, Corporate Accounting Practices. In this position, Frank had to keep himself informed on all new accounting practices and make sure that all of the Cramer accounting procedures were updated regularly. In order to do this it was necessary for him to spend most of his day reading and writing procedures. He had very little personal contact with others.

Several months after Frank's appointment, the president of the company had received several complaints from clients, who said that Cramer accounting procedures were not being updated in accordance with previous policy.

When he thought about this situation, Cramer realized that the complaints had started shortly after Frank's promotion. Cramer decided to review Frank's personnel records. There he found performance reviews made by Frank's previous supervisors, and the comment about Frank's aptitude for dealing with people. Cramer decided to have a talk with Frank about his present work.

During the meeting with Frank, Cramer noted that Frank seemed much more interested in people than he was in procedures. This reinforced the previous supervisor's comments. As a perceptive manager, Cramer realized that Frank's promotion, while deserved, nevertheless had placed him in a slot which made it virtually impossible for him to utilize his major strength: dealing with people. Cramer then decided to offer Frank the opportunity to take over as supervisor of the Accounts Receivable section, which employed a large number of clerks who required a great deal of personal attention. Frank responded enthusiastically to this suggestion. A month after Frank had been on the new job, Cramer was pleased to hear that things were going more smoothly than ever in the Accounts Receivable Department.

Here, a perceptive manager identified and utilized the strength of a capable employee. As a result of building on strength instead of focusing on weakness, everyone involved became a winner. It doesn't require much perception to guess what the ultimate outcome could have been had Cramer left Frank in Corporate Accounting Practices.

Now let's take a look at another situation, in which a manager who was not perceptive unwittingly contributed to a problem.

Floyd Scott was the Midwest regional sales

manager of a very large company. Ron Madison had just been promoted to the job of Wichita sales manager in Floyd's region.

Prior to this promotion, Ron had been an outstanding salesman in the Western region. Not only had he won Salesman of the Year Award two years in a row, he had increased sales in his territory by 217 percent. When his promotion to sales manager was announced, the company organized a special farewell luncheon. Many of Ron's customers were invited, and all made a point of saying how much they had enjoyed doing business with Ron.

Before Ron arrived on the job in Wichita, he met with Floyd in the Chicago regional headquarters. It was made clear to Ron that as sales manager his main responsibility would be to keep Floyd informed of everything that happened in his district. Floyd expected Ron to submit weekly reports on sales, expenses, new customers, product inventory, auto mileage, etc. It was imperative that these reports be on Floyd's desk every Monday morning. Furthermore, Floyd said, Ron should be available in his office in Wichita in case Floyd needed to reach him by phone.

How do you think this situation worked out? It never did, because Floyd concentrated on Ron's weaknesses rather than his strengths.

From the very first week, Ron was late with his reports. When Floyd called to ask why the reports were late, Ron's secretary told him that Ron was out playing golf with an important customer. Floyd was furious. Six months later, the problem was worse, and Floyd's frustration continued.

Why? Ron's job, as Floyd had set it up, did not

permit Ron to use his great strengths: working with people instead of paper. As a result, both Floyd and Ron as well as customers and other employees came into contact with losers.

THE EMPLOYEE'S VIEWPOINT

Bob Pena was administrative assistant to Wayne Lindsay, Vice-President, Eastern Operations. Wayne had been on the job for only a few months. His predecessor had been a meticulous executive who paid a great deal of attention to the details of the job—but neglected the overall, long-range planning aspects; the work had proceeded without direction. As a result, several serious problems had arisen. When asked how he was going to handle them, Wayne's predecessor had replied, "I'm so swamped now that, even working nights and weekends, I can't catch up on all the paperwork."

Wayne was promoted into this job in the hope that he would be able to save a situation that was fast becoming desperate; he had always enjoyed a reputation for being able to see the big picture, leaving details to detail-oriented people. But he inherited so much scrambled detail work that he was uncertain about how to proceed. His perceptive administrative assistant, Bob Pena, saw that his new boss was getting bogged down in minutiae, and that his talents for long-range planning were being wasted.

Under Wayne's predecessor, Bob's own natural ability for details had been underutilized, and he had become frustrated. When Wayne took over Bob recognized that here was an opportunity for him as well as for his new boss. If Bob could take over some of the details that plagued Wayne, then Wayne could devote his attention to the planning aspect of the job—so long neglected, so much needed, and made to order for Wayne.

Bob volunteered to see to details, and several months later Wayne was happily able to leave minor decisions to Bob while he focused on policy planning.

By identifying and building on his own and another person's strengths, Bob created a win-win situation. Both he and his boss could function effectively in their own particular areas of ability.

Another example is Howard Peterson, the foreman responsible for construction of the new Westwood Towers apartments. Howard's job was to supervise the project and make sure that it proceeded on schedule. This required a great deal of mechanical know-how.

Don Hendricks was one of the assistants in the architectural firm that designed the Westwood Towers. One of Don's strengths was mechanical know-how, and he loved to get out of his office, away from the paperwork and out to the job site. He tried to do this as often as possible, because, as he often said, "I love to get my hands on the job and get involved in the actual construction. It really makes me feel great." Don spent a lot of time working at the site, and offered Howard many excellent suggestions.

Unfortunately, Howard was not perceptive. He rejected Don's know-how and ideas, and viewed Don as a potential threat to his own niche in the company. As a result of the lack of understanding between the two—and the constant bickering that resulted—the project fell behind schedule.

Had Howard seen Don's strengths for what they really were and allowed them a positive outlet on the job, he could have created a win-win situation. Instead, he concentrated on Don's weaknesses, and both men lost.

Now let's see how a perceptive employee identified her supervisor's strength and was able to create a better work environment.

Shirley Lovejoy was a clerk who worked for Thelma Piller, supervisor of the department. Since Thelma's department was the largest user of supplies, part of her job was to purchase office supplies and equipment. She also did the buying for several other departments.

Shirley was very perceptive, and had noticed that one of Thelma's strengths was in the area of cost effectiveness. Before Thelma had taken over, the supply room was badly managed, and there was a great deal of waste. Thelma was appointed to the job because she was known to be careful with supplies. To cut down waste, Thelma asked other departments to cut their orders to a minimum. She kept her own inventories at a level below the minimum required for smooth operation.

Soon, several commonly used items were out of stock, and people were kept idle waiting for replacement materials—which often had to be rush-ordered on an emergency basis. These delays naturally irritated the other department heads, and a certain amount of friction developed between them and Thelma.

Shirley saw what was going on. She knew that Thelma's talent for conserving materials was a strength, and ultimately beneficial to the company, if only it could be properly directed. In a private talk, Shirley suggested several innovative ideas that would not only help Thelma cut down on waste but would allow her to plan more efficiently for her inventory. She showed Thelma a way to estimate the needs of the various departments thirty days in advance, to avoid costly rush orders. Quantity orders for some items also proved to be very worthwhile and money-saving.

Thelma was delighted to accept Shirley's help, because she could see that by implementing these ideas she would make the operation more cost-effective. By allowing Thelma to use her strengths, Shirley was able to control the supply problem—which in turn reduced the friction between department heads. Result: another win-win situation.

It's obvious that when a person can utilize his strengths on the job, he is more effective and probably more satisfied. Where circumstances do not allow a person to use his strengths, he makes changes in the way he does the job, becomes frustrated and loses interest in the work—or finds a way to utilize his strengths outside the job.

Often, people ask: What does my employee—or my boss—do wrong, and how can I correct it? A better question is: What does he do uncommonly well? The first focuses on the negative. The latter is a platform to build upon.

We've all heard the statement "You learn from your mistakes." There's truth in the statement, but we also learn from what we do right. Being aware of this can make a big difference when you deal with people's strengths.

5. UNDERSTANDING AND SATISFYING
INDIVIDUAL HUMAN NEEDS

MANY BOOKS on management-employee relationships refer to human needs. They are classified in different ways and under many different headings. Some place these needs in a hierarchy, or define them as job-related or non-job-related. Often the same need is called by different names. Some books claim there are only three basic human needs; others say there are fifteen or more.

In the Open Management System we are concerned with five *basic* human needs which incorporate numerous others. They are psychological, rather than physical needs (such as food, water, shelter, and so forth). It is understood that unless basic physical needs are satisfied, one cannot survive, and that until they are met nothing else matters. In other words, man does not live by bread alone—unless there is no bread.

In the Open Management System we assume that these basic physical needs are being satisfied and, therefore, something more is required. "Something more" refers to universal psychological needs—basic needs felt by everyone, though not always to the same degree.

We can define these psychologically as:

1. *The need for Economic Security.*
2. *The need to Control.*
3. *The need for Recognition.*
4. *The need for Feelings of Personal Self-worth.*
5. *The need to Belong.*

Just as physical needs must be met if one is to live, so too must psychological human needs be satisfied if one is to live meaningfully and with a sense of purpose. If these needs can be satisfied on the job, the work will be enriched. If they are not satisfied on the job, the individual will attempt to satisfy them off the job, and the work will remain boring, frustrating, meaningless.

Usually the means for satisfying physical needs are found on the job. Unfortunately, psychological or human needs often are not.

But people work just as hard to satisfy human needs as they do to satisfy physical needs. At work, both managers and employees are motivated when they recognize that the job can help meet some of the individual human needs.

As noted earlier, the five basic human needs are

felt by everyone, but normally one of them predominates. Some people are motivated primarily by a need for economic security; in others, the need to control might be strongest.

Since work satisfaction depends to a great degree on whether or not strongly felt needs are being met on the job, it's important to know which needs are prime motivators. It's possible to identify the needs that predominate within any one individual by observing that person's traits and attitudes.

The Need for Economic Security

The man or woman with a very strong need for economic security is often characterized by the following:

• demonstrates maximum interest in the security represented by money

• directs efforts toward maintaining job security

• avoids situations which threaten economic security

• gives careful thought to even small expenditures of money

• often dampens efforts of associates who threaten his economic security

• very interested in financial benefits, bonus plans, stock-purchase plans, retirement plans, recreational programs, etc.

• may be willing to mark time on the job to maintain his economic security

• will continue to work at a job he doesn't enjoy if pay is good

• interested in monetary accomplishments

• takes great pride in making financial investments for the future

• accepts the profit motive as the basis for industry and as a legitimate organization purpose

• prefers goals to be realistic, attainable, and related to financial accomplishments

• works aggressively toward removing barriers to financial goals

• tends to work well in a profit-oriented environment

• demonstrates continued interest in financial matters even as wealth accumulates

• strongly influenced by the security represented by financial worth

• demonstrates low regard for those who spend money indiscriminately

• very interested in making money

• very interested in saving money

The Need to Control

The man or woman with a very strong need to control is often characterized by the following traits and attitudes:

• likes to be in charge of any activity in which he is involved

• seeks position of authority and wants to remain in this position

• feels a need to plan, direct, and control other people's lives

• gets things done, meets schedules and quotas

• establishes goals and tells subordinates how to get there; does not tolerate disagreement

• expects obedience to authority and rarely asks subordinates for advice; establishes clear lines of accountability

• does not like to have his decisions questioned

• expects subordinates to follow through on his decisions

• intolerant of errors; tends to blame people for mistakes

• does not accept excuses

• welcomes direct confrontations

• likes to win arguments

• utilizes meetings to state views; believes he is usually right

• likes to run his own shop

• likes to demonstrate his ability to get results

• demonstrates ability to lead and shows strong initiative

• makes periodic, unannounced inspections; favors the military approach

• likes to prove the rightness of his position

• has strong convictions

• becomes overly concerned with need to keep busy

• desires to master his environment

• likes to have things done his way

The Need for Recognition

The man or woman with a very strong need for recognition is often characterized by the following traits and attitudes:

• likes to be the center of attention

- welcomes every opportunity to gain additional recognition
- avoids situations where his achievements cannot be recognized
- needs recognition reinforced regularly, perhaps several times a day
- seeks praise consistently
- needs to feel appreciated
- seeks rewards for personal accomplishments
- likes to display status symbolism in an ostentatious manner
- is conscious of appearance
- wears the "right" clothes for purposes of recognition
- talks loudly
- readily accepts praise
- needs to believe that his accomplishments are considered important by others
- creates conditions where his contribution is recognized
- desires involvement and responsibilities which provide recognition
- sets specific goals which, when achieved, will provide recognition
- welcomes job assignments that provide recognition
- strives for fame

The Need for Feelings of Personal Self-worth

The man or woman with a very strong need to feel self-worthy is often characterized by the following traits and attitudes:

- wants regular reassurance that his personal worthiness is appreciated
- requires conditions which reinforce his feeling of being wanted by others
- avoids situations which disturb the status quo
- avoids conflicts or encounters which threaten his feeling of personal security
- accepts unpleasant tasks if personal security is enhanced
- tends to be loyal
- makes few demands on others unless his personal security is threatened
- likes to have people think well of him
- directs creativity toward developing situations in which personal security will be enhanced
- may accept compromise situations if the feeling of personal self-worth is enhanced by so doing
- tries to fulfill needs of others to increase feelings of personal self-worth
- reports all news to boss and subordinates in order to gain feeling of personal security
- prefers the role of "good guy"
- believes he must do what others regard as the "right" thing
- seeks the approval of others
- is concerned about the opinions of others
- needs the feeling that he is making a contribution

The Need to Belong

The man or woman with a very strong need to belong is often characterized by the following traits and attitudes:

- demonstrates concern for people in the group he identifies with
- feels attitudes of people in his group are important
- follows the crowd
- seeks to gain acceptance from others in the group
- avoids conflicts
- tries to overlook faults of others in the group
- seeks to avoid rejection by the group at all costs
- takes pride in long service with groups he associates with
- aims for sociability and harmonious relationships within the group
- shares thoughts with others in the group
- avoids situations which will result in strained relations within the group
- avoids behavior that would set him apart from the group
- stifles individuality in favor of conformity
- follows fashion and fads set by the group
- enjoys being with people in the group
- conforms to traditions of the group
- is a "team player" and very cooperative
- accepts a problem as his if it is a group problem
- is impressed by membership in certain organizations

You may have noted some similarities in the traits and attitudes that characterize the five human needs; many do overlap, and show themselves in similar ways.

In reality the five needs are interrelated and not distinctly separated, as we have described them, but for purposes of clarification we have defined each as if it were distinct and separate.

Again, each person will have one, sometimes two, needs more strongly felt than the rest. Each need within each person might be described as being a minimum need, an average need, or a maximum need. The range of human needs can be indicated graphically, as in Figure 8.

PROFILE OF HUMAN NEEDS

Observed Range

Human Needs	Minimum	Average	Maximum
Need for Economic Security	___/	_____	__/_
Need to Control	_/_	_____	__/
Need for Recognition	_____	_____	_/_
Need for Personal Self-worth	_____	__/_	_/_
Need to Belong	_____	_/_	_____

Figure 8

Let's consider some examples of how a profile can be used to identify which needs predominate in a particular person.

Phil was very concerned about losing his job. He usually brought his lunch to work and ate at his desk. He wore the same plain suit to work every day. He drove a ten-year-old sedan. In his conversation with fellow employees he often offered comments about the amount of money he was saving for retirement.

From these clues the perceptive observer could certainly identify Phil's strongest human need as the need for ecomonic security. The profile of human needs that might be plotted for Phil is shown in Figure 9.

PHIL'S PROFILE OF HUMAN NEEDS

Observed Range

Human Needs	Minimum	Average	Maximum
Need for Economic Security			x
Need to Control	x		
Need for Recognition	x		
Need for Personal Self-worth	x		
Need to Belong	x		

Figure 9

Because economic security was Phil's priority human need, it had to be met on a continuing basis if Phil was to enjoy satisfaction in his work. (The other needs are shown as minimum because we have no facts about them.)

Keep in mind that Phil's profile is based on information that was available to all who took the trouble to watch and listen to Phil—which is why this approach to identifying human needs is so valuable: Any perceptive observer can use it.

Let's take a look at someone else now. Agnes wanted to take charge of every activity in which she was involved. She regularly told others what to do, how to do it, and when to do it. She expected to have people do things her way, and they usually did if they wanted to get along with her. At meetings Agnes always sat near the front if possible, and did not hesitate to express her views.

From this evidence we could identify Agnes's strongest human need as the need to control. The profile of human needs for Agnes is shown in Figure 10.

AGNES'S PROFILE OF HUMAN NEEDS

Observed Range

Human Needs	Minimum	Average	Maximum
Need for Economic Security	X		
Need to Control			X
Need for Recognition	X		
Need for Personal Self-worth	X		
Need to Belong	X		

Figure 10

The process of actually filling in a profile helps to point one's thinking in the accurate directions. With a bit of practice, the technique becomes an easy-to-use and efficient tool for working with people. The profile approach also provides a graphic representation of a person's needs, and is a ready indicator of those that require maximum attention.

Now for a few more examples:

Fred wanted to be the center of attention in his activities. He constantly sought praise for his actions. He liked to be complimented on his clothing. He talked loudly and with authority within groups. He was not above calling attention to his accomplishments. He responded very well to praise.

From this pattern the perceptive observer could easily identify Fred's strongest human need as the need for recognition. The profile of human needs for Fred is shown in Figure 11.

FRED'S PROFILE OF HUMAN NEEDS

Observed Range

Human Needs	Minimum	Average	Maximum
Need for Economic Security	x		
Need to Control	x		
Need for Recognition			x
Need for Personal Self-worth	x		
Need to Belong	x		

Figure 11

Many people tend to pass judgment as to whether a particular maximum need is "good" or "bad." This should always be avoided. The point is not whether one likes or dislikes an individual and his behavior, but to discover what needs motivate his actions and thus gain insight into what he requires to feel real on-the-job satisfaction.

It is equally important to be objective and keep the other person's point of view in mind while attempting to identify his primary needs. In other words, try to step out of yourself for the time being, suspending both your own point of view and any tendency you might have to make value judgments about the other person's needs.

Here are two more examples of how to use the profile approach: Milton sought constant reassurance that his work was appreciated. He liked to have people think well of him. He was cooperative with his co-workers because he wished them to think highly of him. He frequently asked his boss whether he was satisfied with his work.

From this we could be reasonably sure that Milton's strongest human need was the need for feeling personal self-worth. Milton's profile of human needs is shown in Figure 12.

MILTON'S PROFILE OF HUMAN NEEDS

Observed Range

Human Needs	Minimum	Average	Maximum
Need for Economic Security	x		
Need to Control	x		
Need for Recognition	x		
Need for Personal Self-worth			x
Need to Belong	x		

Figure 12

Sally had a high concern for people in the group she identified with. She went out of her way to gain their acceptance. She tried hard to avoid behavior which would set her apart from the group. She often talked about the organizations and clubs to which she belonged.

From this we could make the assumption that Sally's strongest human need was the need to belong. Sally's profile of human needs is shown in Figure 13.

SALLY'S PROFILE OF HUMAN NEEDS

Observed Range

Human Needs	Minimum	Average	Maximum
Need for Economic Security	x		
Need to Control	x		
Need for Recognition	x		
Need for Personal Self-worth	x		
Need to Belong			x

Figure 13

Again, the whole point of identifying primary human needs is to create conditions that lead to satisfaction on the job. If an individual's maximum human needs can be met on the job, he will find the work meaningful and fulfilling. If these needs are ignored, the job will be boring and the work will suffer.

The following examples illustrate—from the manager's viewpoint—the third principle of the Open Management System: Understand and satisfy individual human needs.

The Case of the Low-price Buyer

Bob Dickerson was an assistant buyer with the Cameo Electronics Company, one of the fastest-growing companies in a fast-growing industry. Cameo's young president, Tom Hayward, had a business philosophy which he expressed often and loudly: "If you want to make money, you've got to spend it." He believed in going first class all the way, and this included buying only the highest-quality equipment and supplies. He wanted his philosophy understood and acted upon by all his employees.

But Dickerson believed in buying from the low bidder. To him a penny saved was a penny earned. Bob lived modestly, even though he earned a good salary and could have afforded a more luxurious lifestyle. He frequently brought his lunch to work. He sincerely believed that everyone wants to buy at the lowest possible price. "It only makes good sense." On one occasion he remarked to another buyer, "The boss will really be pleased to hear how much money I saved the company this month because I bought X from the low bidder. So I had to sacrifice a little on quality. But the price was right."

Tom Hayward knew that Bob was not purchasing top-quality products, and saw this as a potential source of problems. As a perceptive employer, he also knew that understanding Bob's maximum human need was the key to creating a satisfactory work environment for Bob. From observing Bob, Tom was able to identify Bob's maximum human need—obviously, the need for economic security.

As a result of plotting a profile of Bob's human needs, Tom realized that his own policy of "spending money to make money" ran counter to Bob's strongest-felt need. In thinking about it Tom concluded that he would have to try to make Bob see how, in the long run, he would be saving even more money by adopting Tom's policies, and that he would thereby gain even greater economic security.

"What Do You Think You're Doing?"

Tony Frazer was the office manager of the Weston branch of the Capital City Bank. Many of his people were uncooperative, and there was a lack of motivation in the department. There was also a high rate of turnover.

Several incidents involving Frazer and his subordinates were circulated along the office grapevine.

There was the time when he made a clerk resubmit an entire credit report became of a couple of spelling errors. On another occasion, when a clerk suggested a way to increase efficiency in his area, Frazer told him, "What do you think you're doing? When there's a better way to do it, I'll let you know." His demand that all letters and reports cross his desk (he usually red-penciled them and returned them to be rewritten) was a constant source of irritation.

Tony's boss, George Meloun, the branch manager, was concerned because of the high turnover and the dissatisfaction in Tony's department. George decided to call Tony into his office and set him straight on how to run his department. During the meeting, George made it clear that he expected Tony to adhere to standard-practice rules even more closely than in the past. He told Tony to reduce personnel turnover in his department—or there would be severe repercussions. Tony did not respond well to George's remarks.

A month later, George was very disappointed and angry to learn that the turnover in Tony's department was as high as ever, and that complaints had actually increased.

It was evident from Tony's behavior that he had a

maximum human need to control a situation from his own point of view. George would have seen this if only he had taken the time to understand Tony. But instead, George's insistence that Tony follow standard company rules left Tony with nothing to control; Tony's maximum need was not satisfied on the job, and the result was frustration for Tony and even greater problems for his department. Everyone lost.

The Case of the New-Accounts Clerk

Brian Latour was a Customer Accounts supervisor in the Westdale branch of Hobson's Department Store, where he had been employed for sixteen years. Brian had worked his way up through the ranks, and had held his present job for seven years.

Latour's section had the reputation of being a results-oriented group. One of the best people in the section was young Conrad Ellington, the New Accounts clerk. Conrad had been with Hobson's for four years, and was considered a hard-working young man with outstanding potential. Recently, however, Brian had noted that Conrad's performance had dropped off and that, in fact, he was doing a barely minimum job.

When Brian asked Conrad if anything was bothering him, Conrad replied, "Nothing's wrong, Brian, but the way I see it, my job just isn't very important."

Several months before, Conrad had suggested to Brian that the group might operate more efficiently if Brian would allow Conrad to assign the various new accounts to other departments for processing. Brian said that this would not be necessary; that he would continue to handle that part of the job himself.

Brian had not recognized Conrad's maximum human need. If he had been more observant, and if he had done a profile of Conrad's human needs, he would have seen that for Conrad recognition was of prime importance.

But Brian operated in such a way that Conrad got little recognition for his suggestions and was not allowed to implement his own plans. Thus, Conrad's maximum need went unsatisfied. So long as Brian withheld recognition from Conrad, Conrad remained dissatisfied —and the lose-lose situation continued.

The Case of the Cautious Clerk

Bill Harendon was a payroll clerk for Hollybush Construction Company. He had been doing a good job for sixteen years. Every eighteen months he was appraised according to company policy, and got the standard cost-of-living increase. His performance record was generally very good.

Nevertheless, Bill seemed to lack drive and initiative. Each day he called some of his old friends in the company to find out how they handled various problems related to company policy. He was always anxious to let them know how he felt about the good old days, when everything was less complicated. Invariably he was told, "Bill, your records are always correct. Keep up the good work."

It had been noted that Bill wasted many hours each week in checking over every payroll record two or three times—probably because several years ago he had made a serious mistake and been severely reprimanded by his supervisor. He constantly asked his present supervisor, "How am I doing?"

When a new computerized information system was introduced, Bill strongly resisted the change. He was heard to say several times, "I don't think I can ever get used to this new way of doing things."

Bill's supervisor, Glen Lasky, was very concerned about having the computerized information system accepted by the members of his group. He knew that Bill, because of his seniority in the group, could influence the others to accept the system. Through close observation, Glen saw that Bill's maximum human need was for feelings of personal self-worth, and that he viewed the computerized information system as a threat.

Because he didn't understand—or trust—the system and how it worked, he feared a repeat of his unfortunate experience of a few years back when he had been reprimanded for a serious payroll error. In other words, Bill saw the system as something that might diminish rather than enhance his feelings of personal self-worth.

Glen took Bill aside and explained that the new system was more thorough and accurate than the old one. He encouraged Bill to investigate the checks for accuracy that were built into the system which made it virtually mistake-proof. By so doing, Bill was convinced that the system could be trusted and posed no threats—that with it, in fact, he could feel more confident than ever before.

Glen Lasky chose an approach that satisfied Bill's maximum human need. When Bill accepted the new computer system, his co-workers, too, went along with the change. Of course, the company heads were also pleased with the smooth transition to the new system, and the result was an all-around win-win situation. Everyone gained.

The Case of the Head Clerk

Louise Watkins was head office clerk at division headquarters of the Greenwood Engineering Company. Each year the division vice-president invited his key people to a backyard barbecue at his home. Louise was never invited, and was obviously unhappy about it. She always asked what went on, who was there, and what was said. She became impatient and short with the people around her after these parties, and her effectiveness was greatly reduced.

Louise was proud of her company's twenty-year bracelet, and wore it every day. She also wore a service-club pin, and on her desk was a picture of the bowling team she belonged to. Once, at the service club, Louise mentioned that at a recent luncheon the president of Greenwood Engineering had told her that Greenwood was planning a substantial expansion program; what Louise neglected to say was that this was at the annual employees' luncheon, and more than four hundred people were present. Louise often wasted her own time (and the time of others) complaining about office cliques.

Louise's supervisor, Marilyn DeWitt, was concerned about the way Louise spent her time complaining—which not only interfered with Louise's work but also with the work of others. Marilyn recognized from what she had seen and heard that Louise's maximum human need was the need to belong.

Marilyn also realized that when this strong need

was not satisfied Louise was frustrated and difficult to work with. To help her, Marilyn decided that Louise would be the ideal person to arrange office retirement lunches, service-award ceremonies, and similar office functions. In this way Louise's need for belonging was satisfied: She was part of many necessary groups within the organization. Marilyn felt, and rightly so, that in taking these positive steps Louise would be less inclined to waste her time complaining.

Once again a perceptive manager created a win-win situation for everyone's benefit.

To summarize: By stopping, looking, and listening, the perceptive manager can identify the maximum human need of individual employees. When attention is directed to creating an environment in which the maximum human need can be satisfied, the employee is more highly motivated and happier on the job. He feels like a winner. At the same time the manager (as well as the company) is also a winner.

Now let's see how the third principle of OMS works from the employee's point of view.

The Case of the Reluctant Manager

Roy Armstrong was the manager of the Long Range Planning Department. Roy used office equipment until it was completely worn out. This meant that the Long Range Planning Department had to function with some rather antiquated equipment. Roy had been heard to say, "My job is to keep our costs down and to save every penny possible. One of the best ways to do this is to use equipment for as long as possible."

The unfortunate result of this philosophy was that

the people in Roy's department often lacked the proper equipment to do their jobs.

Janice Murray was a planning analyst in Roy's department. Janice realized that Roy's policy of using equipment until it failed might not be so very economical after all. Newer equipment would have allowed the department to keep pace with the new demands that were made on it. Because of the old equipment, many of the Long Range Planning studies were behind schedule.

Roy gave very careful consideration to even the smallest expenditure. He double-checked every requisition. He frequently talked about the importance of investing for the future, and was known to have made several wise and profitable investments.

Janice was concerned about the fact that the Long Range Planning Department was getting further and further behind in its studies. She recognized that Roy's maximum human need was for economic security. Realizing the necessity for more modern equipment in the department, Janice decided to talk to Roy and present the subject to Roy in a way that would make him see the long-term economic gains in time and money as outweighing the original cost. Roy was pleased with Janice's ideas because they satisfied his need for economic security. Janice was pleased because she got the new equipment, and the company gained through increased output from the department. Thus, another win-win situation.

"Always Check with Me First"

Gordon Fitch was supervisor of Field Service Representatives. Gordon required each of the service representatives to check back with him on every deviation from the standard operating procedure, no matter how insignificant. This policy left no room for flexibility on the part of the field service representatives. Often this resulted in delays in servicing and repairs of customers' equipment, which was both costly and annoying to the customers. Turnover in Gordon's department was high.

Ted Peterson was one of Gordon's field service representatives. Recently Ted was out on an emergency job. Contrary to standard practice, Ted allowed the customer to borrow a piece of equipment. Ted tried to check with Gordon but was unable to reach him, so he went ahead on his own. When Gordon heard about this, he was annoyed with Ted and told him, "Always check with me first!"

Ted saw that it was important to include greater flexibility in the standard practice and allow the field service representatives more authority in emergency situations. A very perceptive observer, Ted recognized that Gordon's maximum need was the need to be in control. He further understood that if the standard practices were to be changed, Gordon would have to do the changing. Therefore, Ted indirectly suggested that Gordon expand the original procedures—which Gordon himself had written—to include the broader emergency procedures. Ted convinced Gordon that by making the change he would have even broader control over what each of the field service representatives did and be able to exercise it in a much greater variety of situations.

Ted created a favorable environment for his boss to satisfy his maximum human need. Ted also saw Gordon's need to be in control as a strength, and encouraged him to use it more effectively on the job. Result: a win-win situation for all concerned.

The Case of the Disappointed Secretary

Irma McClean, the administrative assistant to Lloyd Stevens, also supervised the small office staff. Lloyd was involved in many community activities: chairman of the Chamber of Commerce, past president of a local service club, chairman of the Centennial Committee. He was also an active fund raiser on his church's building committee.

Lloyd was district manager for the Smith Company, but he prefered to spend his time with the various groups which gave him recognition, and so he delegated most administrative details to Irma.

Irma felt that Lloyd should handle many of these management tasks himself. She politely told him that she was getting bogged down in her own work because she had to handle so much of his work with customers. Irma recommended to Lloyd that he devote more attention to budgeting and Advance Customer Account planning rather than spend so much time on his community involvements.

Irma was distressed when Lloyd did not respond well to her suggestions. Instead, he spent even more time away from the office. This left Irma with an even greater number of details to attend to.

If Irma had been more perceptive and plotted Lloyd's profile of human needs, she would have seen that Lloyd's maximum need was for recognition. Because she didn't do this, she had no way of knowing why Lloyd did not respond favorably to her suggestion, which, from

Irma's point of view, seemed very fair. But from Lloyd's point of view, following Irma's advice only threatened to reduce the recognition provided by his outside activities. So Irma lost.

"I Don't Have All the Facts Yet"

Frank Mason was credit manager of the Eastbrook Department Store. One of his responsibilities was to decide which past-due accounts should be maintained and which ones closed. Ed Pollack, the Eastbrook bookkeeper, was concerned about the number of accounts that Frank allowed to remain open. Ed felt that if a bill went unpaid for over ninety days no further credit should be extended. Often Frank did not agree. Frank told Ed on occasion, "I don't have all the facts yet. There may be a good reason why the payment is delayed, and I don't want to lose a good account."

Ed knew that many of these overdue accounts would have to be written off, and that the company would only lose more money if they were not closed.

Frank believed strongly in trying to help people. He worked hard to cooperate with others. When confronted with a decision, he shied away from doing anything that might make him look unworthy to others. It was well known at Eastbrook that once, when Frank had to decide about taking on an additional cashier, he took so long to make up his mind that the best candidate took a job elsewhere.

Ed decided to make up a report to show Frank the real cost to the company of extending further credit to poor risks. Frank thanked Ed for the report and said he would take it home to study. Several months passed, and

Ed heard nothing from Frank about the credit report. Frank continued to allow long-past-due accounts to remain open.

Ed's basic mistake was that he did not recognize that, over and above everything else, Frank's basic need was to feel good about himself. Ed's report, which emphasized the economic factors, did not do anything to satisfy Frank's maximum need for feelings of personal self-worth. This is why it was rejected.

The Management Committee

Phil Mahoney was a Commercial Services manager, with his company for thirty-two years. He regularly associated with a group of other managers who had worked together for twenty or more years. They lunched together, and frequently their relationships extended outside the office. In general, they were all conservative in their decisions, and they worked well together. Before deciding anything on his own, Phil always gave serious consideration to what his group would think.

Dave Jennings, a Commercial Service representative in Phil's department, came up with a plan for reducing customer call-backs and speeding up refunds. He spent a long time working up the details of his plan. When he was finished, Dave's facts and figures made it obvious that if the changes were initiated the company would gain.

Since Dave knew that Phil was strongly influenced by the management group, he suggested that Phil refer the plan to the group and set up a review committee. Phil was receptive to the idea of setting up a committee composed of his own management group, and acted on the suggestion promptly. Shortly thereafter, Dave was pleased to learn that the committee had approved the new plan.

It was evident to Dave that Phil's maximum need was to belong. Acting on his observation, his plan was presented in such a way that Phil could see how it could be implemented without threatening his feeling of belonging to the management group.

By identifying and then satisfying another person's maximum human need, a more favorable work environment is created. On the other hand, an environment that thwarts satisfaction of the need is unfavorable. In such an environment, the work is a source of frustration, anxiety, or boredom—a way to earn a paycheck, nothing more.

The five basic human needs we have been discussing here are felt in varying degrees by everyone. People are motivated by the possibility of satisfying them. In effect, all action stems from these attempts. So often we ask ourselves why a person acts in a certain way. The answer is obvious: to satisfy his needs.

One of the underlying concepts of Open Management is that every person is unique unto himself and has every right to personal privacy. Therefore, neither managers nor employees should play the role of the spy who goes about with a little black book making notes of what others do or say, and then reading too much into it. Open Management is an open and aboveboard relationship between any two people. Anything beyond that is a misuse of the concepts.

In the Open Management system, the human symbols that are discussed are the symbols that people wish others to see and hear, and they are seen and heard. Open Management encourages in both managers and employees a positive active awareness of what is going on about them constantly. The objective of this positive active awareness is to develop understanding of the other person's viewpoint, strengths, and human needs. While people are not completely aware of why they display their human symbols, nevertheless they do so very openly.

No surreptitiousness is involved. For example, a person who has a strong need to belong to a particular group does whatever will insure being well regarded by this group. The symbols he displays in actions or words are *openly* displayed so that the group will continue to accept him. He may not be aware that he is doing the things he is doing and saying the things he is saying for need satisfaction; nonetheless, they are being done openly rather than secretly, and there is no invasion of privacy.

The perceptive observer needs only to interpret what is there for everyone to see and hear, what everyone does see and hear, but very few understand.

One of the great contributions of Open Management is that it clarifies a complicated subject, one usually so shrouded in technical jargon and sophisticated terms that no one recognizes the relationship between the concepts and their own job. Open Management bridges the gap between the theory and its technical aspects, and the practical needs of managers and employees on the job.

A word of caution. Since it is virtually impossible to be objective about oneself, we should keep in mind that a person should avoid trying to analyze his own needs from his own symbols, but rather to use the approach with other people. Remember: "The lawyer who hires himself has a fool for a client."

The guidelines discussed in depth in Chapter 8 were developed specifically to help managers and employees to "read" and interpret human symbols in a meaningful way.

OMS is definitely not manipulative. While one could manipulate another person through this approach, it would only be a short time before the other person became aware of the fact that he was being used, which creates a self-defeating, win-lose situation. Open Management helps both managers and employees to realize that in the win-win situation both have the most to gain. This is definitely not manipulation.

So while manipulation may seem to provide satisfaction to one of the people involved, the feeling is only temporary. As soon as the other person realizes what has taken place, the effectiveness is lost, probably forever.

One of the reasons why there is such concern about manipulation is that all too often in the past many techniques for working with people have stressed such aspects as more productivity, and little thought has been given to individual human needs; so, much latent suspicion exists. OMS, however, is not a manipulative approach because manipulation by its very definition implies a gain for one at the expense of another. In the win-win approach this does not happen.

6. THE CIRCLE OF REFERENCE

So far we've discussed three principles of the Open Management System:

1. *See a situation from the other person's point of view.*

2. *Identify and build on individual strengths.*

3. *Understand and satisfy human needs.*

The interrelationship of these three Open Management principles has a synergistic effect; their collective practical application results in a work environment in which optimum motivational conditions exist. But how to apply them collectively? The OMS includes a concept called the "circle of reference," a very valuable tool that assists in the practical application of all three OMS principles.

We can think of the Circle of Reference as being made up of three parts: self-image, human symbols, and human needs (Figure 14).

The Self-image

Each person has a self-image. Through his own eyes he sees himself in various ways. For example, one person may see herself as successful, honest, intelligent, trustworthy, and hard-working.

An understanding of self-images is a great help in working with people. A person will be receptive to anything that reinforces or enhances a positive self-image. Anything that threatens the self-image will be resisted.

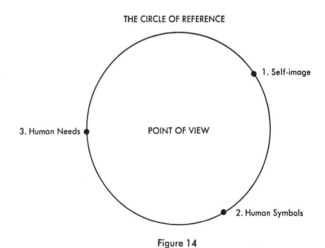

THE CIRCLE OF REFERENCE

1. Self-image

3. Human Needs   POINT OF VIEW

2. Human Symbols

Figure 14

A manager who thinks of himself as a friendly person will respond favorably to those who treat him as though he were friendly. An employee who sees himself as being loyal to his employer will respond favorably to those situations in which he is treated as a loyal employee.

Conversely, a manager whose self-image is that of a competent person will feel threatened by—and resist—situations in which he is treated as incompetent. An employee whose self-image is that of a punctual person will feel threatened by—and resist—situations in which he is treated as lacking in punctuality.

Many people understand the importance of the self-image in creating a favorable work environment, but doubt their own ability to recognize how others see themselves. Actually we are all able to identify and enhance each other's self-images, and in fact we do it successfully almost all the time. We know this because 90 percent of the time people get along with one another, which means they reinforce each other's self-images; at the very least, they coexist. The question arises, why is it important to spend time discussing this subject if we get along with people 90 percent of the time? The answer, of course, is that during that 10 percent of the time in which we do not get along with others, 90 percent of our problems are created.

Just as some people doubt their ability to recognize self-images, others may object to the idea of doing the "amateur-psychologist bit." "Psyching people out," they feel—playing to another person's self-image—is not only manipulative, but also potentially harmful. To this, we can only say that, as with many tools, working with the self-image can indeed be dangerous. But, as with a saw or a chisel, it can also be made to work *for* us when used under safe working conditions. Certain guidelines are essential to working with tools, and practice increases proficiency. So it is too when one works with self-images. With guidelines for proper usage, self-images are safe and useful tools for working with people.

What are the guidelines? They come with the recognition of human symbols and the understanding of human needs.

Recognizing Human Symbols

What a person says and does, as well as the material things with which he surrounds himself, are all symbols of his lifestyle. Recognition of the true meaning of these symbols is of great value to any person seeking to understand others.

A manager who displays his golf trophies at the office almost certainly has an image of himself as a capable golfer and would like his co-workers to share this viewpoint.

An employee who decorates his work area with certificates of achievement and talks about his accomplishments probably has an image of himself as a capable and hard-working person. He too would like his co-workers to share this viewpoint.

Understanding Human Needs

These are the same human needs discussed previously in Chapter 5.

That same manager who has an image of himself as an outstanding golfer and surrounds himself with golfing trophies responds well to statements or actions which satisfy his need for recognition as an outstanding golfer. The trophies are only a symbol of the need for recognition.

The employee who displays his certificates of achievement and talks about his accomplishments responds well to statements or actions which satisfy his need for recognition as a capable and hard-working person. Here again, the certificates are only symbols of the need for recognition.

The human symbol, then, is a visible or audible guideline to understanding the human needs of the individual. The human need in turn is a guideline to recognizing the self-image. A significant relationship exists between these three points. An understanding of this relationship helps one to work competently and confidently with the self-image.

7. THE SELF-IMAGE—
IDENTIFYING SELF-IMAGE FORMS

THE SELF-IMAGE is the first point on the Circle of Reference.

"Self-image" is a psychological term with many meanings. Consequently, it is often misused and misunderstood. In this chapter we will explore the meaning of the term as it applies to the OMS, along with practical ways in which the concept can be utilized in working with people.

An individual's self-image is formed in earliest childhood. As the person grows, the self develops and is molded by all the outside influences with which it comes into contact. Parents, teachers, peers, and other people, as well as events and situations, all help to shape the self-image. A woman who grew up in a wartime environment has been strongly influenced by the war—even though she may not have been personally involved in the war itself, she has been shaped by what she saw and heard others talking about, as well as by specific situations.

A person growing up during a severe depression is affected by the environment as well as the people with whom he comes into contact. A happy vacation time or a pleasant event at school can be powerfully influential in shaping an individual's self-image.

In working with people it is important to understand the impact of these influences on the individual. A particular event or situation can affect different people in different ways. A move from one town to another, for example, might help one child become stronger and more self-reliant. The same move might contribute to feelings of insecurity and lack of self-confidence in his brother.

Events and situations continue to shape the self-image, but by the time a person reaches the business world his self-image is fairly well established, and it, in turn, influences the way he interprets and reacts to events and situations.

Therefore, if you want to know why a person does the things he does, and says the things he says, you have to understand his self-image. In fact, the more one understands about another person's self-image, the more one will be able to understand the reasons for his actions.

In dealing with another person we often find ourselves relating to that person in one particular role. For instance, we may see the woman who lives next door as a neighbor and never perceive her in any other way. Our entire relationship is that of neighbor to neighbor. But if we wanted to improve the relationship, it would be helpful to be able to see her as a whole person, rather than deal with just that part of her that we perceive as "neighbor."

The whole person is actually made up of many persons, and each represents the whole at a particular time. It could be said that every one of us is actually many people—each of whom is complete unto himself. The interesting point is that the sum total of all these many people that make up the whole is more than the sum of the separate persons. The concept is analagous to a melody. It is made up of a series of individual notes that, when played, has a richness and meaning that is more than just the sum of its notes. (In the same way, it is like a book, which is more than its words. Or a word, which is more than its letters.)

Each person lives a variety of different roles, and in trying to develop rapport or understanding it is important to be aware of the whole person *and* the various roles that make up the whole.

In Figure 15, for example, at least six separate roles make up the whole person. (It should be understood that there could just as well be more or fewer roles than shown. We have indicated this by "others" in the circle.)

One role of the whole person has to do with the family. Each of us is a member of at least one family: the family into which we were born. Most of us are members of several families: our parents', our own, our in-laws', our children's, etc.

THE WHOLE PERSON
Various Life Roles

Figure 15

Another role is the one played out in the community. Again, each of us lives somewhere. The location may or may not be the same as the one in which one works. The relationship of a person within the community also affects the others.

We all have some kind of social role, which is influenced by the way we live, our recreational activities, our relations with neighbors, the clubs and organizations we belong to, and so forth.

Then there is a political role, a spiritual role, and, of course, the role played out on the job.

Many people spend more time in one particular role than in others. For example, a person can become so immersed in his job role that all other roles are of less importance. This is shown graphically in Figure 16.

THE WHOLE PERSON
Job Role of Maximum Importance

Figure 16

The person represented in Figure 16 is so taken up with his job and its related activities that his other life roles are minimized; his interest, time, and attention are concentrated on the needs of the job. Decisions involving the individual's other life roles are probably made with reference as to how they will affect the job role. In choosing whether to spend time on the job or elsewhere, the job will win out.

Individual life roles naturally vary for each person. Further, they may change over the years. New roles may appear, and existing roles may diminish or disappear.

In identifying an individual's self-image, it is important to understand the whole person and the relationship of the various roles that exist within that whole person. (We can liken the process to working a puzzle; we cannot complete the picture unless we have all the pieces—but, more than that, we must be able to place each piece in its proper place.) We must also remember that each person views himself in a unique way, and that to understand him requires an understanding of the way he sees himself.

To work effectively with another person, it is necessary not only to understand but to reinforce the self-image. Any threat to the self-image, either real or imagined, will be resisted, and the greater the threat, the greater the resistance. Reinforcing or enhancing the self-image works in the opposite way.

When a particular action is interpreted as being threatening, a negative feeling results. The self-image is diminished or subtracted from. The action itself is negative, or nonreinforcing. As a result of the negative action, one feels less good about oneself as a person. When an action is interpreted as self-enhancing, positive feelings result. The self-image is built up or added to. It is reinforced. In other words, positive feelings come about when an action is accepted as reinforcing. As a result of positive actions, one feels good about oneself as a person.

Whether a particular action is interpreted as positive or negative depends on the person to whom the action is directed. (In other words, two different people may view the same action in two different ways.) The only way to know just how a particular individual will interpret a situation or event is to try to view it from his or her point of view.

To better understand the self-image it is necessary to recognize that for everyone it exists in two modes: the way a person sees himself, both now and in the future, and the way a person wants other people to see him. While it can be argued that there are still other modes of self-image, these two are the ones with which we concern ourselves in the Open Management System.

First, let's examine the way a person sees himself, now and in the future. In this mode of the self-image, a person sees himself as he believes himself to be. For instance, a man who has children may see himself as an excellent father. Another person, observing his actions and hearing his words, may indeed share this image that he is a good father. Anything said or done that supports this man's image of himself as a good father will be well received. Any words or actions that threaten the image will be resisted.

A manager who sees himself as well-organized and efficient will respond well to comments and actions which support his self-image. Threatening words and actions will be resisted.

An employee who sees himself as hard-working will respond well to comments and actions which support this image. He will resist any words or actions which threaten his self-image.

However, a person may see himself differently from the way others perceive him. The manager who sees himself as well-organized and efficient may in fact be incompetent. Nevertheless, a person who wishes to work with this manager will find it necessary to enhance the self-image that he has of himself. Any words and actions that hint at his incompetence as a manager will be seen as threats.

In the same way, the employee who sees himself as hard-working may in fact make very poor use of his time. Nevertheless, a person who wishes to work with this employee will also find it necessary to enhance the self-image that he has of himself. Any suggestion, even though it may be grounded on observable fact, that he is not a hard worker will be seen as a threat.

This is so because for everyone the self-image is so basic and important, and so much a part of every person, that any real or imagined threat to it will be defended. Techniques for defending the self-image are known as defense mechanisms. They protect the self-image in much the same way that actual physical defenses protect the body against physical threats from the outside. In both cases, the mechanism is automatic and spontaneous.

How, then, can a person enhance another's self-image if he doesn't agree with it? One must just try to understand the situation and see the self-image from the other person's viewpoint. In order to do this, it's necessary to look for the things that individual does right and well, and see these as strengths. The strengths then become a sincere approach to enhancing the other's self-image.

An important corollary is that almost everybody tends to see himself as competent in what he does for a living.

A waitress probably has an image of herself as a *good* waitress. She feels this way in order to protect and build her own self-image. She may indeed be a good waitress, and will certainly respond to positive comments and actions that enhance her self-image. On the other hand, even if she is a lousy waitress she will still have an image of herself as a good waitress and will therefore respond to words and actions that reinforce her self-image.

If she is inattentive, forgets your order, and never does get around to bringing your coffee, and you treat her poorly, you threaten her self-image and she will respond in a defensive manner. If one wishes to get along with this waitress, or anyone else, it is necessary to note what it is she does well and build on this in a positive way.

In almost all instances, both on the job and off, people tend to see themselves as good or competent in what they do. To get along with them, one must always enhance the self-image.

As we have said, people see themselves both as they are now and as they would like to be in the future. The implication, of course, is that we all would like to be something in the future that we are not today. A man may have an image of himself as being a good father now but see himself as an even better father as time goes on. A woman might see herself as an excellent secretary today but envision herself a top-notch administrator in the future.

If it is true that everyone wants to become something other than what they are today, what about the people who are content in their present jobs and have no desire to do anything else?

A person can indeed be content or satisfied with what he is doing now. When one has achieved on-the-job satisfaction, one's image of oneself in the future is different in areas unrelated to work. For example, the manager who is content to remain in the small branch office may see himself in the future as a better golfer or a better husband, or as president of the chamber of commerce. The employee who is content to be a telephone operator may have a future image of herself as a better artist, a better mother, or a pilot

Like the present self-image, the future self-image may or may not be a realistic one. The manager who saw himself as president of the chamber of commerce may have an exaggerated opinion of his own ability to function in this position. The employee who saw herself as an artist may have unrealistic expectations about her talent as a painter.

The point is: In learning to work with people, it is important to understand that—just as in the case of the present self-image—the future self-image must be enhanced and not threatened. Words and actions that reinforce the manager's future image of himself as president of the chamber of commerce will be well received. Anything which is perceived as being negative or threatening to the future self-image will be resisted.

The self-image is particularly sensitive to words and deeds that seem to ridicule or poke fun at it. Again, this is true of both the present self-image and the future self-image, and regardless of whether the ridicule is real or imagined. The favorable work environment has no room for ridicule. But in order to know what comments or actions might be interpreted as ridicule, it is necessary to see the situation from the other's point of view.

The future self-image can be enhanced in much the same way as the present self-image. Sincerity is important, but one needn't jeopardize one's personal integrity. Once again, the key is to build on strengths, and to keep the other person's point of view firmly in mind.

Of course, some people have rather low images of themselves. In order for them to improve their own images they tear down or depreciate the self-images of others. Their hope in doing so is that their own images will seem better by comparison.

In addition to the way we see ourselves now and in the future, another mode of self is present in everyone; it has to do with the way we want others to see us. In other words, we want people to see us doing and hear us saying the things that we wish to be seen doing and wish to be heard saying.

For instance, a manager working busily at his desk may be seen by many people—including his boss, his co-workers, and his employees. These others are seeing him as he wants to be seen, and this is reinforcing to his own self-image. But it may be upsetting if someone happens to catch him reading a sports magazine in his office if this is not the way he wishes to be seen by others.

Similarly, an employee who is chatting casually with another about the latest TV show when the supervisor happens by may be disturbed if this is not the way he wishes to be seen by his supervisor. (If such is the case, he will probably stop talking and return to his work immediately, because he wishes to be seen doing the things he wishes to be seen doing.)

In still another instance, it may be upsetting to a particular manager if someone happens to see him reading a business newspaper at his desk, if this is not the way he wishes to be seen. But another manager may be delighted to have others see him reading business newspapers, because he wants everyone to view him as a person who keeps himself well-informed.

Here are a few more examples illustrating the first principle of the Open Management System—that of seeing a situation from the other person's point of view—and indicating how and why it so often happens that the image one wishes to project may not be viewed by others in the same way. Consider the manager who regularly takes work home. He may want others to think of him as a hard-working, dedicated person who devotes many hours of personal time to his job. Some of the people who see him doing this will see him as he wants to be seen and admire him. Others may see him simply as a person who does not spend enough time with his family.

Or consider the employee who works late. He may wish to project an image of himself as an especially conscientious person. If his boss happens to see him at his desk after normal closing time, he may indeed view him as an industrious worker. On the other hand, the boss might wonder why this employee can't get the job done during regular working hours.

William Shakespeare had a fine understanding of the concept of the self-image. In *As You Like It*, he says:

> All the world's a stage,
> And all the men and women merely players.
> They have their exits and their entrances;
> And one man in his time plays many parts

William Saroyan recognized the concept of the projected self-image when he wrote, "Life is but a stage on which each of us tries to give his best performance."

THE MANAGER'S VIEWPOINT

Lee Stanton was an office manager. His young clerk, Bob Buckner, was an outstanding employee. Bob was competent and well-liked and worked hard at his job. He was cooperative and willing to take on new assignments and responsibilities. It was obvious that Bob wanted to get ahead.

Bob had an image of himself as a conscientious and dedicated employee. He saw himself as a future manager, and wanted others to think of him as a person with the potential and desire to be a manager.

Lee was perceptive and understood Bob's image of

himself. Lee viewed Bob's self-image as a realistic one, and recognized Bob's future potential. Lee knew that if he reinforced Bob's self-image, Bob would be pleased, and so he seized every opportunity to do so. He truly felt that Bob would be able to take on a supervisor's responsibilities in the near future.

As a result of this approach, Bob was even more highly motivated, and handled his present job with greater efficiency and skill.

Don Meyer was another office manager. Steve Pearson, a young clerk, was a member of Don's work group. Steve was an average performer. He did only a fair job, and spent much time trying to figure out how to avoid certain responsibilities. The general feeling within the group was that Steve was only barely competent.

However, Steve's own image of himself was that of a capable, efficient person. He felt certain that he would move ahead in the company. Steve wanted others to see him as a future manager.

Don, concerned about Steve's poor performance, invited him to discuss the matter. During the interview, Steve remarked that he viewed his present job as being only a temporary situation and that he would soon move up the ladder into a supervisory position. When Don heard this he laughed and told Steve, "You don't have a chance of being promoted. If you don't shape up and start doing a better job, you may not even be working here."

After the interview, Steve seemed very depressed. Several weeks passed, during which Don noted that Steve's level of performance had dropped even more. Don never understood why this should be so.

Obviously, Don did not share or even recognize Steve's image of himself. When he laughed at Steve and downgraded his abilities, Steve's self-image was seriously threatened. Steve had to go on the defensive to protect it. Unless Don begins to understand and enhance Steve's self-image, the situation will probably worsen.

Sal Maloney was another office manager who had a young clerk, Nancy Morganstern, in his work group. Nancy, too, was an average performer. Her output was only fair. She wasted a lot of time talking about non-job-related activities. Her fellow employees liked her but didn't see her as having management potential.

However, Nancy saw herself as efficient and capable. She wanted to be promoted to a supervisory position, and often talked about the changes she would make when she had the authority.

Sal knew that Nancy had genuine ability to handle disgruntled and irate customers, and wanted to help her develop her potential. As a perceptive manager, Sal realized that Nancy viewed herself as a future supervisor and that she wanted others to see her in this same way. Therefore, Sal reinforced the image that Nancy had, by allowing her to spend more time doing the things that she did best. He emphasized her strengths and enhanced her self-image, and soon Sal was pleased to note that Nancy's performance was steadily improving.

Sal was successful in working with Nancy because he did not threaten her self-image. He identified her strengths and reinforced the image she wished to project.

THE EMPLOYEE'S VIEWPOINT

Gil Haskell was a computer programmer. His boss, Art Miley, was a hard-working manager, good at following directions but often hesitant about making decisions without first getting approval.

Art had an image of himself as a conscientious and

dedicated worker who is fair and considerate of others. He wanted others to think of him as an effective manager.

Gil understood Art's self-image, and recognized it as realistic. Gil also saw that sometimes Art was hesitant about making decisions on his own authority—which often delayed Gil in his own work.

Gil knew that if he could enhance Art's self-image, Art would be pleased, so Gil made the most of every opportunity to reinforce the way Art saw himself. He did this sincerely, because he felt that Art would be able to develop confidence in his own decisions if his self-image were enhanced. As a result, Gil noticed that Art had become less hesitant to make decisions than before.

Gwen Nolan, a saleswoman, worked for Alice Dougherty, a realtor for over twenty-five years who appeared set in her ways of doing business and reluctant to accept suggestions for change.

Alice's self-image was that of a successful leader in the real-estate business. She wanted others to see her as a realtor offering courteous, dependable service.

Gwen wanted Alice to accept some new approaches to selling homes—but to Gwen's suggestions Alice replied, "I've been doing business my way since before you were born, and I don't plan to change now."

Following that confrontation, none of Gwen's suggestions was implemented. Gwen could not understand why Alice did not accept her ideas.

It is apparent that Gwen did not understand Alice's self-image and how she wished others to see her. When Gwen suggested that Alice change, she was in effect threatening Alice's self-image. This might have been anticipated by a more perceptive employee, but unfortunately Gwen did not recognize how Alice saw herself, nor did she make an attempt to see the situation from Alice's viewpoint.

Alice and Gwen both lost.

Rick Richardson was a draftsman for Stan Nettlewick, the drafting supervisor, who was a neat, meticulous, and well-organized person who paid a great deal of attention to details.

Stan had an image of himself as a careful planner who avoided mistakes by thinking ahead. He wanted others to see him as well-organized and careful to avoid unnecessary risks.

Rick thought he could benefit from Stan's talent for planning and organizing, and realized that in order to accomplish this he had to enhance Stan's self-image. So Rick took every opportunity to do so. He was sincere in this, because he truly believed that Stan was a good planner and that he could learn from Stan's experience. As a result, Stan was very willing to share his experience with Rick.

Understanding self-images is one of the key factors in understanding people and the Open Management System, and the concept applies equally to both managers and employees.

Some people carry pictures of their loved ones in their wallets or purses. But we all carry pictures of ourselves in our minds. The better we can see the picture that other people have of themselves, the closer we come to understanding them.

Often these pictures, or self-images, are vague and difficult to identify. This has always been a problem for both managers and employees. In the next chapter, "Recognizing Human Symbols," new ways to identify self-images are discussed.

8. RECOGNIZING HUMAN SYMBOLS

EACH PERSON surrounds himself with things that represent the image he has of himself, as well as the image he wants others to see. These things, or symbols, also indicate how an individual's human needs can be satisfied; they are, in fact, tangible evidence of both an individual's self-image and the needs which he seeks to satisfy. Anyone can learn to recognize human symbols; they are there for all to see.

We are all familiar with the term "status symbol," which usually refers to such ostentatious displays as expensive automobiles, large houses, luxurious furnishings, and extravagant clothes or jewelry. The term "human symbol" is much broader; it includes the just-mentioned status symbols, but much more as well.

Suppose you are in a shoe store, watching the customers. Three pairs of shoes, all similarly priced and similar in style and color, are on display. A buyer enters and looks at the shoes. Let's assume that all would look appropriate at his job, as well as to his family. When a final choice is made, the buyer will probably select the pair which pleases him most.

Why? The buyer liked the style, the color, and the price. No doubt about it. But why? Something within him made an evaluation, and he responded accordingly. He liked what he bought best because it satisfied his need and enhanced his self-image. If he were asked the question "Why did you buy that particular shoe?" he might speak about price, color, and style. But the truth lies deep within himself, and he probably couldn't put it into words. This is where symbols are of great value to the perceptive observer. The answer to the question "Why did you buy it?" is not as important as seeing that he did buy it. Obviously, it *represents* something to him.

Now suppose that a second buyer enters the store and sees the same three pairs of shoes. When he makes a final choice, the second buyer has selected a different pair.

Why did the first buyer select one pair of shoes and the second buyer select a different pair? Because each is a unique human being. Each has a different background and different past experiences, and has been conditioned by different influences. Each has a different image of himself. Each selected the pair of shoes which best enhanced his self-image.

So the first ground rule of observing human symbols is:

In general people will accept, buy, and surround themselves with things they like rather than things they dislike.

This rule may seem too obvious to mention, but it cannot go unstated. If a person buys and accepts what he likes, then what he buys and accepts will provide clues to his self-image and human needs.

The term "human symbols" includes not only those things already mentioned as status symbols, as well as jobs, clothing, homes, cars, but actions, mannerisms (including gestures), and speech. Actually, everything, big or small, can be seen as a human symbol.

Often symbols are thought of as being only tangible or material things. But the things that people talk about, the words they choose, and the way they use them are also symbols. This brings us to our second rule:

When given the opportunity, people usually talk about themselves or the things that interest them.

This too seems to be a statement of the obvious, but it is a significant point. Why? Because words are symbols of our thoughts and the way we regard ourselves. Words provide further clues to the individual's self-image and human needs. The keen observer must also be a good listener. To develop good relationships with people, it is necessary to watch and listen for the human symbols.

For example, Susan likes to wear brightly colored clothes. Seeing Susan's brightly colored clothing, we might assume that Susan has an image of herself as attractive, and that she wants others to see her in this same way; also, that she wishes to stand out from the crowd and be noticed (or that Susan has a strong need for recognition).

In a restaurant, Philip was heard shouting loudly at his children, "Hurry up, I've got to catch a plane." Hearing Philip's outburst, we might assume that he has an image of himself as important and wants others to see him in the same way. We might also assume that Philip has a strong need to be in control of situations.

Michael was seen eating his lunch at his desk one day, and was heard to say "The price of eating out at a restaurant today is ridiculous." We might assume from his words and actions that Michael has an image of himself as a thrifty person and wants others to see him this way. We might also assume that Michael has a strong need for economic security.

By being able to interpret symbols, we can get valuable insight into a person's self-image and human needs. However, additional guidelines are essential. The third guideline for interpreting human symbols is:

Symbols must be seen and evaluated from the other person's point of view.

In the example of Susan's brightly colored clothes, one must decide what they mean to Susan rather than to oneself. Susan may indeed see herself as attractive and want others to share her opinion, and she may indeed have a need for recognition.

But another girl wearing brightly colored clothes may wear them for entirely different reasons. She may regard herself as very plain and wear bright colors so that others will not notice this. She may have a strong need for personal self-worth.

Still another girl may wear brightly colored clothes because that is what everyone else in the office wears. She may see herself as part of a group and have a strong need to belong.

The point, of course, is to emphasize the importance of always keeping rule #3 in mind; symbols must be interpreted from the other person's point of view.

Now for the fourth guideline for interpreting human symbols:

Before attempting an interpretation, look for evidence of a pattern to the human symbols that apply to the individual one is trying to understand.

Susan's brightly colored clothes were viewed as clues to her self-image and greatest human need. Upon closer observation, it was noted that she drives a sporty yellow car and frequently speaks of herself as a rising executive. She often wears flashy rings, bracelets, and necklaces. She lives in a new, fashionable apartment and likes to be seen at prestigious social events, and her picture appears in the society and business sections of the local newspapers.

A pattern emerges from this constellation of human symbols, and it becomes apparent that the original interpretation of Susan's self-image as attractive (and her greatest human need as that for recognition) is undoubtedly correct.

How does one find a pattern of symbols? The answer is: Stop, look, and listen. The symbols are there for all to see and hear—and most people do see and hear them. But many are not aware of their significance. Symbols tell a lot about other people, and the perceptive observer will see the relationship between symbols, self-images, and maximum human needs.

To be a perceptive observer, incidentally, one does not have to stoop to nosing around in other people's private affairs. Far from it. It is necessary only to have a conscious awareness of the symbols surrounding the person one is trying to understand.

Let's go back to the example of Philip, who voiced impatience in the restaurant. His loud comments constitute only one human symbol. Further observation uncovered a pattern of symbols indicating that the original interpretation was incorrect. Philip sees himself as a quiet, family-oriented, thoughtful, and caring person. His maximum human need is more correctly identified as personal self-worth. All this becomes evident when Philip's human symbols are considered as a pattern. For example, in the office he is usually quiet and considerate. He often speaks fondly of his wife and children. He and his family spend many weekends camping together. His car is a three-year-old station wagon; his home is modest. He is active in Scouting and church activities.

This pattern contradicts the original interpretation, which was based on one isolated incident. Without a pattern of symbols, the observer is easily misled.

The fifth guideline in interpreting human symbols is:

Be flexible and avoid making judgments about the value of another person's human symbols.

Symbols are never "good" or "bad," and to judge them as one or the other is to jeopardize one's chances of making accurate interpretations. Rather, symbols should be regarded as mere indicators of self-images and maximum human needs.

THE MANAGER'S VIEWPOINT

The guidelines for recognizing and interpreting human symbols are tools for understanding and working with people, and valuable to any manager seeking to create a better work environment.

In the business world human symbols are particularly visible and audible. Human symbols in business and industry include the size and type of office, its location and furnishings, carpeting, name on the door, private secretary, use of company car, title, immediate supervisor, number of people reporting to the individual and *their* titles, salary, etc.

By interpreting these symbols and many others, a manager can learn how a particular employee sees himself, what his self-image is, and what maximum human needs he has. Symbols, when properly interpreted, can be an excellent basis for developing rapport with an employee or another manager, and are excellent indicators of another person's interests and, thus, his strengths.

The perceptive manager must cultivate flexibility in dealing with his employees. In an attempt to achieve rapport with an employee, one may have had great success in discussing the employee's weekend golf game, for example. On another occasion that same employee may resent any reference to golf; his attitude is different at that particular moment. Thus, timing is important. And so is flexibility. The manager who listens closely and observes carefully will know when and when not to discuss golf.

What about an apparent lack of symbols? A manager may try to understand a particular employee but may find no symbols by which to be guided. Actually, a paucity of symbols is a symbol in itself. A man whose office has no pictures, no ornaments, and no books is providing symbols of his self-image and his human needs that are as visible (and useful) to the perceptive manager as the office filled with symbols.

The following examples indicate how the guidelines for intepreting human symbols are applied in actual business situations.

Andrew:

Eric Fenton was manager of the Design Engineering Section of Dameron Industries. One of his draftsmen, Andrew Goff, had been with Dameron Industries for fourteen years. For the last six years, he had been responsible for the design of all housings for the S-12 line of power drills.

Eric's section was selected to design a new line of combination power tools. Everyone in the section was required to take on a new assignment. Eric was aware of the important role he played in effecting a smooth changeover. He also knew that by interpreting human symbols he would be able to identify each employee's self-image and indicate ways to satisfy maximum human needs. By observing symbols, Eric hoped to obtain clues that would help him to create the conditions for the change-over to take place quickly and efficiently.

Eric noted that Andrew always arrived early and was one of the last to leave in the evening, and also that he was very neat about his dress and his work. He once commented to Eric, "I want to be sure I'm doing this the way you want it done." On several occasions he had asked permission to visit the final assembly area to see the completed product. Andrew kept a picture of his wife and children in his work area, and maintained a very quiet lifestyle.

Observing this *pattern of symbols from Andrew's viewpoint,* Eric concluded that Andrew probably saw himself as a careful and accurate designer, and that he wanted others to see him in the same way.

With these symbols in mind, and *without making judgments* about their value, Eric was able to give Andrew a new assignment—designing modified housings—that enabled him to maintain his image as a careful, accurate designer and satisfy his maximum need.

Joanne:

Herbert Steel was manager of the Westbrook Bank. Joanne Randall was one of the employees in the bookkeeping section. Since Joanne's arrival in the section, morale had fallen and productivity had dropped appreciably.

Business was booming, and Herbert realized that something would have to be done to alleviate the problem. He had noticed that Joanne wielded a great deal of influence with others in the group, and therefore he felt that with her cooperation the group's productivity might improve.

In watching and listening to Joanne, he discovered that she often told others what to do, and appeared to direct the activities of her entire office "family." She complained when things were not done her way. She did not hesitate to make decisions and to set her own policies. She had made a point of having her desk moved to the front of the office. She was an officer in the local chapter of the Business Women's Association. In addition, Joanne frequently interrupted conversations, and spoke of the people in her section as "my people."

Once Herbert had decided that Joanne herself was the problem in the section, he summoned her to his office and told her that *he* was in charge of the section and that she had better change her behavior in the office. Herbert was sure that after he had made his point, productivity would improve. But a month later productivity had dropped even more, and morale in the section was even lower.

Herbert's analysis of the situation was faulty: He did not *understand the pattern* of symbols he observed, and so did not understand Joanne's self-image. He made no attempt to *view the situation from Joanne's point of view. He made a judgment* that Joanne's behavior was bad.

A more perceptive manager would have deduced from Joanne's symbols that she had a strong need to control, and that the situation could be enormously improved by putting her in charge of a few specific activities, which would have enhanced her self-image and satisfied her needs.

Once again: Symbols are there for all to see, but their meaning is easily misinterpreted.

Virginia:

Nancy Jensen was manager of the Claims Department of the Oakhurst Insurance Company. Virginia Blair was one of the claims investigators in Nancy's department. Virginia was a reliable investigator, but was almost always late with her follow-up reports. Nancy's job would have been easier if Virginia had been more punctual.

Nancy had observed that Virginia was very active in the company bowling league; her office was filled with the many trophies she had won. On her desk was a picture of herself receiving the Oakhurst Woman of the Year award from the Mayor of Oakhurst. She drove a red convertible, and for the third year in a row had been voted one of the ten best-dressed women in town.

Nancy observed this *pattern of symbols* and *avoided making a judgment* regarding them. Instead, she interpreted these symbols as indicating that Virginia had a strong need for recognition. Nancy decided to initiate a plan that would give Virginia more recognition on the job. Part of her plan included regular meetings with Virginia to discuss follow-up reports. These meetings gave Virginia some of the recognition she needed, and the recognition in turn motivated a desire to get her reports in on time.

In all three cases, the symbols were there for all to spot. Good managers have learned the technique of interpreting their meaning.

THE EMPLOYEE'S VIEWPOINT

Managers, too, manifest patterns of symbols, and the same five guidelines for interpreting them can aid the employee's understanding of the boss.

From these human symbols an employee can learn how a manager sees himself. A perceptive employee might wonder how understanding and interpreting these symbols will help him on the job. The fact is: Symbols, when properly interpreted, are an excellent basis for developing rapport with other employees or with the boss. They also indicate the other person's interests, and give clues as to which actions and topics of discussion should be avoided.

Consider the following examples:

Frank:

Bernard Lacy was an appliance repairman for the Miller Appliance Company. His boss, Frank Miller, was the owner of the company. Bernard was losing valuable work time because of problems with the old company truck he drove, and because Frank did not provide him with the good new tools that would enable him to do better-quality repair work. Bernard was frustrated by this state of affairs, and wanted Frank to shell out for up-to-date equipment.

Bernard, considering the situation, observed that the Miller shop was poorly lighted, and in need of over-all modernization. All of Frank's trucks were old, and breakdowns were frequent. Frank provided his men with the bare minimum in tools. When one of the repairmen complained about this, Frank replied, "You don't need all that fancy stuff. When I started out, I got by with a screwdriver and a pair of pliers." Frank's own car was an eight-year-old panel pickup, and though his income was good, his clothes were shabby.

In recognizing this *pattern of symbols* and what they represented from *Frank's point of view,* Bernard saw that Frank's self-image was that of a thrifty person who abhors waste, and that he had a strong need for economic security.

Bernard decided to demonstrate to Frank that by purchasing modern equipment and overhauling the trucks, his men would be able to complete their repair jobs faster, and the end result would be a more profitable business. Bernard's approach worked, and both men were happier on the job.

Brad:

Gary Dillon was a foreman in the Peabody Works of the Reliable Manufacturing Co. His boss, Brad Hawkins, was superintendent. Gary wanted Brad to approve the installation of a small coffee area on the shop floor so that the men could have a place to relax before work, during breaks, and at lunch. Gary knew the men would appreciate this, and he felt they deserved it because of their excellent performance record over the previous year.

In watching and listening to Brad, he had noted the following pattern of symbols: Brad was a hard worker who had come up through the ranks. He regularly inspected the entire plant, and did not hesitate to give orders directly to the men on the job. He often forgot to tell Gary what he had done. His shirt sleeves were usually rolled up, and he was in the habit of carrying a clipboard, on which he regularly made notes. He brought his lunch, and ate in his office while continuing to work.

His office was plain and without ornamentation. On one occasion, when the discussion turned to improving on-the-job morale, he replied, "People are *paid* to work here; no need to coddle them!"

Gary saw this *pattern of symbols* but did not take *Brad's point of view* into account. In an effort to convince Brad to approve the coffee area, Gary had all the men sign a petition, which he presented to Brad. He was surprised and disappointed when Brad rejected the petition outright, saying, "This is ridiculous. I never needed a special place to drink coffee. What was good enough for me is good enough for them."

Because Gary failed to interpret the symbols from Brad's point of view, he did not realize that Brad's self-image was that of a hard-working man, and that his maximum need was to be in control. Such a personality could hardly be expected to respond favorably to a petition! If Gary had not demanded, but instead had found some way to allow Brad control of the installation of a coffee area, the outcome might have been more positive.

Andrea:

Cheryl Howard was a fashion designer for Christopher Fashion, Inc. Her boss, Andrea Sterling, was manager of Fashion Design for the firm. Cheryl had an idea for a unique design which she believed would be a top seller. She wondered how to get Andrea to approve the design.

Cheryl knew that Andrea was a brilliant design manager. She also was president of the Professional Fashion Design Society. The Society's award for excellence in design was displayed prominently in her office. On her desk was a large picture of herself with Mr. Christopher, president of the company, and on the wall was a photograph of herself modeling one of her most successful designs.

Andrea drove an expensive car; her clothes were always high-style. She dined regularly at the best restaurants. Her home was luxurious, the furnishings exquisite.

Cheryl observed this *pattern of symbols* with *Andrea's viewpoint in mind.* She concluded that Andrea saw herself as a successful, highly competent manager. So, to get her new design approved Cheryl presented it in such a way that Andrea saw it as an opportunity to gain recognition for her own managerial competence. Because the new design originated from Andrea's department, it enhanced Andrea's self-image and provided her with recognition from her boss and the Fashion Design Society.

Human symbols are valuable because they enable one person to perceive the image that another person has of himself. They also indicate the other person's maximum human need. They are nothing less than the keys to understanding people. Perceptive managers and employees will see and hear them in order to find out what needs they are meant to satisfy. Our next chapter will examine the nature of human needs and how they can be satisfied.

9. UNDERSTANDING HUMAN NEEDS

Perceptive Approaches to Human Needs

THE THIRD point on the Circle of Reference is "understanding human needs." As you will recall from Chapter 5, these human needs are:
- the need for Economic Security
- the need to Control
- the need for Recognition
- the need for Feelings of Personal Self-worth
- the need to Belong

Human needs are manifested through human symbols. As discussed in Chapter 8, actions, words, and the things with which one surrounds oneself are all human symbols. The keen observer is able to interpret these symbols and see the relationship between them and the individual's self-image and strongest human needs. In effect, the symbol satisfies the need and at the same time serves to enhance the individual's self-image.

Human needs are recognized only through human symbols. Therefore, in an attempt to create a situation for these needs to be satisfied, one must pay attention to these human symbols—or to the apparent lack of them. Remember: Everyone surrounds himself with human symbols—and a lack of symbols is a symbol in itself.

The OMS approach to understanding human needs through human symbols is based on three guidelines. First: *Though human needs can be identified from human symbols, one symbol may represent different needs to different people.*

In other words, the symbol is only a clue through which a need can be perceived. A person who buys and wears a brightly colored, high-fashion sport coat may do so in order to fit in with the group; if everyone else in his office dresses in this style, he is in keeping with his group. In this case, the coat may symbolize a need to belong.

Another person who buys and wears the same type of coat may be satisfying a need for recognition. Still another person may buy the coat to enhance feelings of personal self-worth; or for economic security; or to satisfy a need to feel in control of a situation.

In order to determine which need is being satisfied, one must look for a *pattern* of symbols, always keeping the other person's point of view in mind.

The second guideline for interpreting human

needs through symbols is: *The human need itself must be satisfied, not the symbol of the need.*

A brightly colored, high-fashion sport coat is significant in terms of what it represents. If the sport coat is a symbol of the person's need to belong, comments that satisfy this need, rather than threaten or ridicule it, will be well received.

A statement such as "Your new sport coat makes you look like one of us" would be well received by the individual with a strong need to belong to a group. The same person might feel threatened by a statement such as "Your new sport coat certainly makes you stand out from the rest of us." This would tend to make a distinction between the person and the group with which he identifies.

Whatever need the sport coat symbolizes, it is a need the individual wishes to have satisfied. Or, as stated in the guideline, the human need itself must be satisfied, not the symbol of the need.

The question one must ask oneself when the goal is to understand another person is: What symbols will best satisfy the need? Obviously, we are not suggesting that the person with a need to belong be presented with a sport coat, but that when one understands the need represented by the sport coat one is in a better position to create situations that satisfy the need.

The symbol and the need it represents are also clues to actions that might be considered threatening and could therefore work against the creation of an aura of understanding.

The third guideline to understanding human needs is: *A symbol not only identifies a human need but contributes to the satisfaction of that same need.*

The fashionable sport coat may be the symbol of

the person's need to belong, but it also helps to satisfy the need. With this concept in mind, one can proceed to find other ways to meet this need.

People often refer to symbols as "my" house, "my" car, "my" job, "my" family, etc. Each of these symbols is regarded by the individual as a part of himself. (Why else would he refer to them as "mine"?) Obviously, then, the more parts or symbols one can identify, the greater the chance that the symbols will be interpreted accurately.

The person who speaks of "my" house, "my" car, "my" job, "my" family is actually saying, "My needs are represented by these things."

The idea that a person's needs are represented by many parts, or symbols, correlates with the concept of the "whole person." The better the whole person is understood, the better his needs will be understood.

At this point, one might ask "Where do human needs come from, and why are there such variations in individual human needs?"

One answer to this highly significant question is: Human needs stem from the individual's self-image.

In the chapter on self-images, two modes of the self were discussed: the way a person sees himself both now and in the future, and the way a person wants other people to see him.

These two different modes are not distinct and separate. Rather, they overlap and are in a state of constant interaction. By the time an individual goes to work, his self-image has been well established. Since human needs stem from the self (or the self-image), it follows that human needs also have been well established by the time a person takes his first job. The relationship between the two—human needs and the self-image—is such that the needs can be satisfied only when the self-image is enhanced.

A more detailed breakdown of the different elements constituting the Circle of Reference is shown in Figure 17.

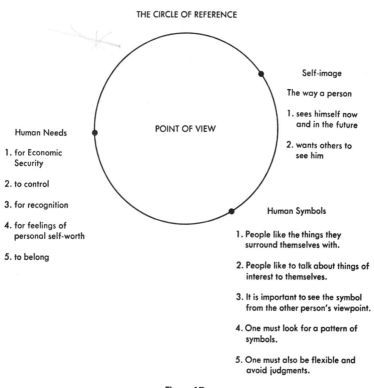

THE CIRCLE OF REFERENCE

POINT OF VIEW

Self-image

The way a person

1. sees himself now and in the future

2. wants others to see him

Human Needs

1. for Economic Security

2. to control

3. for recognition

4. for feelings of personal self-worth

5. to belong

Human Symbols

1. People like the things they surround themselves with.

2. People like to talk about things of interest to themselves.

3. It is important to see the symbol from the other person's viewpoint.

4. One must look for a pattern of symbols.

5. One must also be flexible and avoid judgments.

Figure 17

The Circle of Reference is a tool for developing empathy—an understanding of another person's point of view (the first principle of the Open Management System).

The Circle also illustrates how the area of understanding between two individuals can be enlarged. It emphasizes those aspects of the other person's point of view that one must try to understand in order to create conditions for on-the-job satisfaction. Additionally, the guidelines for using the Circle of Reference indicate how to identify and avoid those situations which might contribute to a separation between two viewpoints. It can therefore be used to minimize the effect of divergent forces, which all too often are in control when one sees a situation only from one's own point of view.

The second principle of the Open Management System stresses identifying and building on individual strengths. As we know, human needs stem from a person's self-image, and by the time a person reaches the business world his self-image is fairly well defined—and therefore his human needs are also well defined. A recognition of this fact is important, since all too often people spend much effort trying to change other people's human needs. To do so is virtually impossible. In the Open Management System, the idea is not to try to change human needs but to channel them into areas where they can be satisfied.

This can be done by applying the second principle of the Open Management System. We do not suggest that human needs can always be equated with strengths, but rather that an environment can be created in which needs can be seen as strengths.

As an example, let's consider an employee who has a maximum need to control. A manager might see this need as "bad"—something that must be squelched. But any efforts to do so will meet with much resistance from the employee. If the manager persists and forces the employee to contain his need, he will find himself with a frustrated employee who constantly seeks alternative outlets to satisfy his need. In many cases, efforts to relieve the frustration will be negatively directed. Human needs *will* be satisfied somehow, so unless the employee's self-image changes, which is unlikely, his needs will remain unchanged and the problem will persist.

As an alternate approach, a perceptive manager is able to identify the employee's maximum human need and recognize that it stems from his self-image and, therefore, will have to be satisfied. Rather than trying to modify or contain the need, he will see it as a potential strength. This is not to say that the need to control (or any other need) is a strength or a weakness in and of itself. It is simply a fact. It exists. Whether it becomes a strength or a weakness depends upon the viewpoints of the people involved. Thus, the first and second principles of the Open Management System are interrelated and synergistic; any need can be seen as a potential strength. When these two Open Management principles are applied, a win-win relationship is almost always the result.

Now, another example of a situation involving human needs. Let's consider an employee whose manager has a maximum need to control. An employee unfamiliar with the principles of OMS might see this maximum need as a weakness—perhaps because the manager never allows the employee to do things on his own, but instead gives step-by-step instructions for all tasks assigned. The employee resents this, does things his own way, and openly defies the manager's instructions. This infuriates the manager, because it threatens his self-image and works against satisfying his own maximum human need. The result? The manager issues even more restrictive orders, and the employee finds himself in a lose-lose situation. The employee loses, because he is saddled with more directives than ever before. But the manager loses, too, because even though he seems to be in control, he feels threatened by the employee's resistance.

A perceptive employee, after having identified the manager's maximum human need, would understand that the need must be satisfied if he is to have a good working relationship, and that by helping to satisfy the need the manager's self-image would also be enhanced.

So, rather than trying to change or overcome the need, he would see it as a potential strength. Using the principles of the Open Management System, the employee would create conditions under which the manager could control—but do it in such a way that the manager would gain confidence in the employee's ability to carry out certain activities himself. The manager's need would be satisfied, since he actually would be controlling. At the same time, the employee would be able to achieve a certain amount of self-determination. By seeing the situation from the other person's point of view and viewing the manager's maximum need as a potential strength, a win-win situation would evolve, and everyone would gain.

In summary: To satisfy human needs and create a win-win situation, several elements must be present. First, the other person's maximum human need must be identified. Second, the need must be satisfied in a way that enhances his self-image. Third, the need-satisfaction must be seen as a potential strength.

In essence, it all boils down to accepting people for what they are. If we could do so, and give up the idea of changing them into what we would like them to become, how much more pleasant and productive all our relationships would be!

THE MANAGER'S VIEWPOINT

The Case of the Cookbook Promotion

Cyril Bradshaw was a Business Development representative for the Westbrook Bank. Above all else, he believes in saving money for the bank. The bank had just initiated a new program designed to increase business, since earnings had been down for the past several quarters. This new Business Development Program was based on giving away a series of attractive full-color cookbooks containing recipes from nations around the world.

The bank spent considerable money promoting these free cookbooks. The campaign, in all the local media, featured the slogan "No obligation—just stop in at one of our offices."

The first results of the program were encouraging. People began coming into the bank in increasing numbers, and many new accounts were opened.

But Cyril believed that since these cookbooks cost money, the bank should be selective about giving them away. Cyril gave the cookbooks only to people who opened new accounts.

The branch manager, Fred Phillips, observed several disgruntled people leaving the bank; Cyril had refused to give them a cookbook, on the grounds that they did not open a new account or already had an account with the Westbrook Bank.

In thinking about the situation, Fred considered what he already knew about Cyril. Cyril had been with the bank for twenty-seven years. He had been assigned his present position to get him out of the way of the bright young executives coming up behind him.

Fred also knew that Cyril drove a seven-year-old car, and that his dress style was several years behind the times. Cyril was once heard to say, "The things people borrow money for these days are ridiculous. Why, just last week a student wanted to borrow money for a vacation! Can you imagine that?"

Recently, when the Westbrook Bank was redecorated and all employees received new modern furniture,

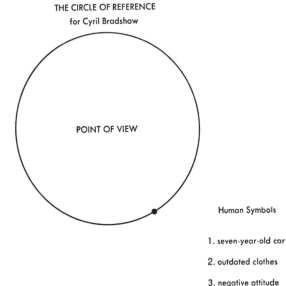

THE CIRCLE OF REFERENCE
for Cyril Bradshaw

POINT OF VIEW

Human Symbols

1. seven-year-old car

2. outdated clothes

3. negative attitude toward how other people spend money

4. feeling that redecorating office is a waste of money

Figure 18

Cyril remarked, "I can't understand why the bank is wasting all this money. My desk is just as good today as it ever was."

Fred wondered what he could do to get Cyril, a loyal employee, good at his job, to cooperate with the new program.

Fred knew how to use the Circle of Reference. He decided to plot Cyril's self-image, his symbols, and his human needs on the Circle. He began with the human symbols with which Cyril surrounded himself, listing them on the Circle of Reference. He did this to gain insight into Cyril's self-image and his maximum human need. (See Figure 18 on page 118.)

From this pattern of symbols—keeping Cyril's viewpoint in mind, and without making a judgment—Fred identified Cyril's maximum human need as the need for economic security. (See Figure 19 on page 120.)

(Of course, Cyril, like all of us, felt other human needs—but to a much lesser degree. In this particular context, they were not significant.)

By watching and listening, Fred also was able to understand Cyril's image of himself, and listed his conclusions on the Circle of Reference. (See Figure 20 on page 121.)

In this way, Fred used the Circle of Reference as a tool for understanding what made Cyril tick. The Circle is a graphic illustration of the relationships between human symbols, human needs, and the self-image. Once these relationships are defined, it is easier to interpret the behavior of any individual. But one must keep in mind that the major function of the Circle of Reference is to determine the strongest human need and how it can be satisfied. Fred was a truly concerned manager, and used

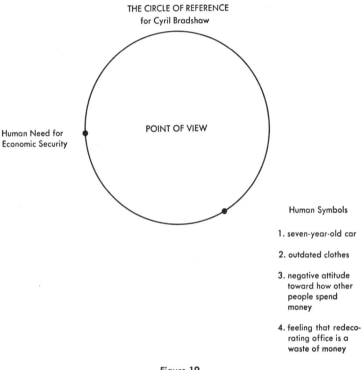

THE CIRCLE OF REFERENCE
for Cyril Bradshaw

POINT OF VIEW

Human Need for
Economic Security

Human Symbols

1. seven-year-old car

2. outdated clothes

3. negative attitude
toward how other
people spend
money

4. feeling that redeco-
rating office is a
waste of money

Figure 19

his new insight into Cyril's character to create a situation
that satisfied his need.

The Creative Employee

Hal Johnson, a former Naval officer, had been
with the Midwest Chemical Co. for four years. During
the past three years Hal had been assistant vice-president
of the Industrial Services Department. He believed in
running his department "like a tight ship."

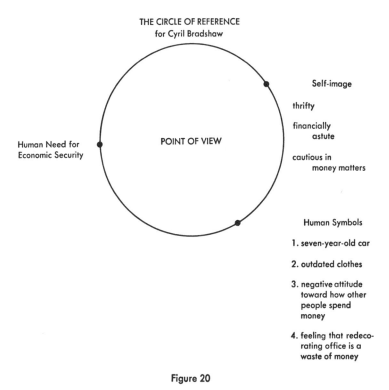

Figure 20

Hal was a stickler for punctuality. If anyone in his department was even a few minutes late coming back from lunch, Hal reprimanded him in full view of the entire group.

One of Hal's men, young Tony Richards, was an extremely creative individual. Tony had been with Midwest Chemical for just a year, yet he had come up with some innovative ideas for changing administrative practices. Many of Tony's ideas had already been put into effect in various departments throughout the company.

Tony's ideas came to him at different times of the day and night. For example, during one lunch hour he had an idea for a new approach to handling an important account. Tony got the whole plan down on paper right there in the restaurant. He was so involved in working out the details that he got back to the office forty-five minutes late. Hal stormed up to him, demanding to know why he was so late. He ended by saying that if it happened again, he would see to it that Tony's services would no longer be needed.

Since then Tony did his work properly, and rarely was late. But his attitude toward the job, the company, and his fellow workers was different, and as a result there were a few personality problems in Hal's department.

Tony wore his hair longer than most of the others in the group. When Hal suggested that he cut his hair shorter, Tony replied, "I'll wear my hair as long as I like!" Tony designed and wore stylish and expensive jewelry in spite of adverse criticism. He preferred to come and go as he pleased, despite the departmental rules.

Hal wondered what he could do to get Tony to conform to the rules of the department.

He was aware of certain symbols, among them Tony's hair style, that he designed and wore expensive jewelry, in spite of adverse criticism, his indifference to departmental rules, his willingness to suggest new ideas.

From this pattern of symbols—and by keeping Tony's viewpoint in mind—Hal should have been able to identify Tony's maximum human need: the need to control. Unfortunately, though, Hal disregarded the symbols as not being very meaningful in terms of Tony's on-the-job activities.

Hal also did not attempt to identify Tony's self-image: that of a creative, forward-thinking, unconventional person.

And so the problem persisted. Tony's indifference to the job was more pronounced, and his attitude contaminated others in the department. Hal was frustrated because his attempts to change Tony were unsuccessful. Midwest Chemical lost, too, because of the inefficiency of Hal's department. Once again, a lose-lose situation resulted from the failure of a manager to recognize the great importance of human symbols and their relationship to human needs.

Why Did She Work So Hard?

Karen Kenwood was a sales-promotion representative for the Wychwood Office Supply Company. Karen had a number of very good ideas to bring in new accounts, and spent much of her own time working out the details. Although some of her suggestions were a bit far out, many of them could have been valuable to the company.

Willard Dolan was the manager of the office where Karen worked. Willard thought that Karen's ideas were ridiculous. As Willard put it, "Some of those harebrained schemes of hers can only lead to trouble. She'd better stop wasting her time with this kind of nonsense and start doing the job she is paid to do, or I'll see to it that she is fired."

Just last month, Karen was instrumental in making the local Camp Fire Girl newspaper drive the greatest success to date. Because of her innovative ideas, there was enough money collected to send three additional Camp Fire Girls to summer camp—a 110 percent increase over the previous year. As a result of her efforts, Karen was named "Woman of the Month" by the local Chamber of Commerce. Karen was working enthusiastically on another community activity, collecting aluminum cans.

Willard noted that in addition to her willingness to offer new ideas, Karen was also a very stylish dresser. She had a personalized license plate for her car with her initials followed by No. 1. She liked to name famous people in her conversation, and leave the impression that she knew them well. She seemed to like being noticed, and responded well to compliments.

From this pattern of sybmols, and by keeping Karen's viewpoint in mind, Willard should have been able to identify Karen's maximum human need: the need for recognition. Unfortunately, Willard was not a perceptive manager. He discounted what he saw and heard about Karen—the symbols—as not being meaningful, and did not see the relationship between them and Karen's job performance.

Further, Willard made no attempt to identify Karen's self-image: that of a hard-working, intelligent, well-organized planner.

So the problem persisted. Karen continued to be deeply involved in her community activities but felt like a loser on the job, because it neither enhanced her self-image nor satisfied her need. Willard was frustrated, because he could not make Karen over into the kind of employee he wanted.

The Man in the Field

Don Osgood was a service representative for United Machinery Corp. He was a long-time employee, well regarded by the company. Some of Don's ideas had become part of the company's service policy.

Don's job had always been a flexible one. He and the other service representatives spent a lot of time out in the field, and generally made their own hours. Don never abused the policy: He was in the office when necessary, and phoned in regularly to check for any calls.

But last year, after a long illness, Don's wife died. Since then he had spent much less time in the office, and sometimes didn't even bother to call in. Recently another service representative saw Don's car parked in front of the Wishing Well Bar at about three o'clock in the afternoon, and just last week a customer reported seeing Don downtown, obviously drunk. The department manager, Bob Larson, wanted to help Don to do the kind of job he used to do.

Bob and Don had worked together for a long time. In addition to being aware of his past performance record, Bob also knew how close Don and his wife were, and how upset Don had been over her death. Don kept a photograph of his daughter and grandchildren on his desk, and carried a similar picture in his wallet. It was generally known that Don wanted to feel that he was making a meaningful contribution to the company.

From this pattern of symbols Bob recognized that Don's maximum human need was for feelings of personal self-worth. He also recognized that Don saw himself as cautious and diligent.

By identifying Don's maximum human need and self-image, Bob was in a better position to understand and empathize with Don. He could take appropriate steps to reinforce Don's self-image and satisfy his maximum human need by creating conditions that would allow Don to feel he was making a worthwhile contribution.

The Old Cliché

Helen Hobson, a secretary in the Trust Division of the Eastwood Bank, was a young, attractive college graduate. She did her job reasonably well. Although she had been with the bank for just a short time, her supervisor felt that she had great potential.

The other secretaries were older and more experienced than Helen. Most of them had been with the bank for more than five years, and knew each other very well. They spent their coffee breaks together, discussing personal as well as bank matters.

At first Helen tried to enter into these conversations, but the other women shunned her. From time to time she made pertinent comments, but got no response other than sarcasm.

One of the women was overheard to say that "people with college degrees think they know it all." None of the other secretaries had a college degree.

Helen's supervisor, Juanita Minton, wanted to help Helen work closer to her potential—but without alienating the other secretaries.

Juanita noticed that Helen still wore her college sorority pin. She made frequent references to the various community groups she had recently joined. To her, "home" was the place where she had grown up, rather than the city where she lived.

From this pattern of symbols—keeping Helen's point of view in mind, and without making a judgment—Juanita concluded that Helen's maximum human need was to belong, and that she saw herself as well liked, cooperative, and a good team worker.

As a result of identifying Helen's maximum human need and self-image, Juanita was in a better position to reinforce her image and satisfy her need to feel a part of her group.

These examples indicate the relationship between human symbols, human needs, the self-image—and how the Circle of Reference helps to keep these principles in mind. In the OMS it is essential for a manager to understand the relationship and its value in creating conditions that lead to satisfaction on the job.

But it is equally important for an employee to be able to see a situation from a manager's point of view, and to understand the relationships illustrated by the Circle of Reference.

THE EMPLOYEE'S VIEWPOINT

"I Always Buy at the Lowest Price"

Phil Sanborn was purchasing manager for the Ironton Insurance Company. Phil loved to tell stories about how he shopped around for months before making a buying decision. Recently Phil spent seven months pondering the details of a new closed-circuit TV for the office security system. The equipment Phil finally purchased was considered an outstanding value for the money spent. Everyone felt he had made the right choice.

Phil was planning to buy new steel furniture for the entire suite of offices. He had been talking with several potential suppliers for more than two months. Phil asked Broderick Simpson, the salesman for Heavy Duty Desk, Inc., for more information about the steel used in the drawers. When Broderick received the inquiry he went to see Phil, and assured him that Heavy Duty used only finest-quality materials.

Broderick knew the following about Phil: He had been in the purchasing department for twenty-four years, and had the reputation of always buying from the lowest bidder. His desk was bare except for two calculators, which he used many times a day. He kept up on all price changes, and was a stickler for details. He never hesitated to ask suppliers for quotations on even the smallest items if he thought that by doing so he could get a better price. When another buyer asked Phil why he worked so hard to save a few pennies, he said, "I always buy at the lowest price. It's worth it to me to make sure that I'm getting the best deal possible."

As a perceptive salesman, Broderick knew he must tailor his sales presentation to satisfy Phil's need. He knew the principles of the OMS, and considered the Circle of Reference a valuable tool in helping to decide how to make a presentation.

Broderick was aware of the importance of human symbols and their role in the Circle of Reference. Thus, he concluded from Phil's symbols—the plain office, the calculators, his reputation for always buying at the lowest price, his penchant for details, the pride he took in his ability to get good deals—that Phil's maximum need was for economic security. Broderick realized that while Phil, like everyone, had all five human needs, this particular need was the strongest.

He made his interpretation while keeping Phil's viewpoint in mind, and without judgment.

Broderick was also able to identify Phil's self-image: Phil saw himself as an astute buyer, hard-working and clever in financial matters.

With this information at hand, Broderick was able to plan a sales presentation particularly suited to convince a potential buyer like Phil that his product provided good value for the money.

Any employee can use the Circle of Reference as a tool with which to reach a better understanding of others, and by following the OMS approach can create an environment for working more effectively with managers and fellow employees. Just as important, the Circle of Reference indicates which actions and words to avoid.

Results Count

Sally Stewart, private secretary to the aging and much-loved president of Easton Supply, J. G. Corning, had been with the company for more than thirty years. J.G. was getting along in years, and did not make decisions as quickly and surely as he used to, so Sally had taken over some of his duties.

Stewart Randolph, the executive vice-president, was expected to replace old J.G. when he retired the next year. Stewart planned to take over many of J.G.'s responsibilities within the next month.

Sally knew that Stewart had a reputation for getting things done. He was comparatively young, having quickly moved up the corporate ladder. He had made significant changes along the way which had improved profits but also troubled a few people within the organization. He was a results-oriented executive who wanted to know only facts.

Once he had shouted at a department head because a simple error had been made. He had often been heard to say, "At Easton we work hard and we play hard." However, no one could remember ever having seen him play.

Sally knew about the significance of human symbols and the role they play in understanding people. She was aware of Stewart's pattern of symbols, and since she expected to be working for him in the near future, she tried to keep his viewpoint in mind and avoid making judgments.

Sally identified Stewart's maximum human need as the need to control. She also identified Stewart's self-image: He saw himself as aggressive, hard-working, serious, and a strong leader.

As a perceptive employee, Sally understood that when Stewart took over from J.G. she would have to enhance his self-image and allow him to satisfy his need to control if harmonious working conditions were to prevail.

A Job Well Done

Al Holland was a programmer in the Electronic Data Processing Division of the Laguna Manufacturing Co. His supervisor, George Knowland, had held his current job for eighteen years. Not long ago George was given a special assignment, which he turned over to Al. Al prepared an outstanding report, and George submitted it to his boss as his own work. Only later did Al learn that George had taken credit for his good work.

Al knew quite a bit about George. He knew that George was a famous college football player, and that in his senior year he scored the winning touchdown which earned his team the State Championship. George frequently recalled this great event. It was known that he kept a scrapbook of newspaper clippings which described his past successes. He invariably showed the scrapbook to visitors. George seemed to get a great deal of satisfaction from talking about the recognition he once received. On the job, however, George had been passed over for promotion on two occasions.

Although Al enjoyed the special assignments George handed over to him, he was upset that George took all the credit. After the latest incident, Al decided to confront George.

He stormed into George's office and told him he could no longer tolerate George's taking credit for his work. George said nothing, and ever since then their relationship was tense. George no longer gave Al any special assignments.

Unfortunately, Al did not recognize George's maximum human needs. The human symbols indicating those needs were there for Al to see—and he did see them, but had no idea of their significance. The symbols, of course, included the scrapbook, and George's reminiscences about his past successes and the recognition he once received.

If Al had understood the meaning of these symbols, he could have identified George's maximum human need for recognition. He would also have been able to recognize that George saw himself as competent but unappreciated—someone who had had a lot of bad breaks.

If Al had been aware of the OMS techniques and had used the Circle of Reference as a guide, he would have known that a confrontation could be interpreted only as a threat to George, and done nothing to enhance his self-image or satisfy his need for recognition.

Al could have approached the situation in a way

to satisfy George's need and at the same time give Al the credit he deserved. Since Al had enjoyed the special assignments, both Al and George lost.

The Case of Millie Schneider

Julia Hoffman was a clerk in the Installment Credit department of a large bank. Her supervisor, Millie Schneider, had been in charge of the department for seventeen years.

Julia was aware that Millie was well liked. Many people wondered why she never had married. On occasion Millie invited some of the other women in the bank to her home. Millie was very interested in her co-workers' personal problems, and was quick to offer advice—usually not the best. Her meddling had caused some problems among several of the employees.

Julia kept her personal life to herself, and did not confide in Millie. So Millie disliked her, and took every opportunity to gossip about her. Naturally, Julia was unhappy about the situation, and decided to tell Millie that she would appreciate it if Millie minded her own business. After this Millie became even more difficult for Julia to deal with.

Julia, unfortunately, did not recognize Millie's maximum human need. The symbols indicating Millie's human needs of course included Millie's all-consuming interest in her job, the fact that she never had married, her intense interest in the problems of her co-workers, and her attempts to solve those problems. Taken together, as a pattern, they pointed to a maximum need for feelings of personal self-worth. Millie saw herself as a person who was helpful to others, and she required regular assurance that she was.

If Julia had been acquainted with the principles of OMS and used the Circle of Reference as a guide, she would have understood that her approach might seem threatening to Millie's self-image and that certainly it did not satisfy Millie's need for personal self-worth.

Julia lost, because she was not able to establish a good working relationship with her supervisor. Millie lost, too, because Julia, unhappy in her work, was not able to develop her potential on the job.

The "In" Organization

Fred Mansfield was manager of the Inventory Control department of the Cedar Grove Distributing Company. Bart Townsend was an inventory-control specialist in Fred's department.

Bart knew that Fred was an active long-time member of the Cedar Grove Club, an exclusive and tightly knit group. This organization was made up of professional men from the area, and one could not join unless recommended by a member in good standing. The club was active in many local affairs, and supported the Community Chest Fund Raising Campaign financially, as well as with man-hours.

At club meetings there was a great deal of free-flowing discussion among the members. A newspaper man was heard to say, "If you really want to know what is going on in this town, you have to belong to the Cedar Grove Club."

Fred was reluctant to do anything that would threaten his membership in the Cedar Grove Club.

Bart was a perceptive person who was aware of OMS principles and realized how the Circle of Reference would help him understand his boss. Specifically, Bart wanted to convince Fred to make certain changes in inventory-control procedures. Fred's symbols indicated to Bart that Fred had a maximum need to belong. Bart also recognized that Fred had an image of himself as a thorough person, happy with the status quo and reluctant to take risks.

So Bart presented his suggestions for changes in a way that threatened neither his feelings of belonging nor his self-image as a careful and thorough manager. Both Fred and Bart were winners.

Understanding human needs is the third element on the Circle of Reference. To sum up, human symbols are indicators of human needs, while the self-image is the "root" from which maximum human needs stem. To work well with people demands an understanding of, and an attempt to satisfy, their human needs.

10. THE MODULE FOR WORKING WITH PEOPLE

So far we have discussed the three basic principles of the Open Management System (see a situation from the other person's point of view; identify and build on individual strengths; and understand and satisfy human needs). However, the Open Management System is not just a theory. It is a *practical approach to working with people.* The value of the OMS is always in direct proportion to a person's ability to use these principles on the job, and a number of techniques have been developed to simplify practical application of OMS.

One of them is the Circle of Reference. Another we call the Module for Working with People (MWP). This technique helps both managers and employees create a positive work environment.

The Module for Working with People consists of three steps, and the first is to determine the performance objective. All too often, people begin a particular job without really knowing or understanding what they wish to accomplish. Unless managers and employees define a performance objective, it is difficult to know if what they are doing is leading them closer to the accomplishment of a task.

Many times people at work are faced with problems that need solutions. It often happens that one knows one must do something about a problem, though what that "something" is remains uncertain. Having a clear idea of the problem requires having a clear idea of the objective—it is necessary to accurately define the problem before one can determine what action to take. If action is taken before the problem is defined, as so often happens, one may never even know whether or not the objective has been reached.

If a person wishes to make more right decisions than wrong decisions, both for himself and for others, he will define objectives for himself and others before taking action.

Objectives can be difficult to define—which is why they are so often ignored or glossed over. In the chapter on setting objectives, you will find some specific guidelines for defining objectives.

The second step in the MWP is identifying individual human needs. Remember that in the Open

Management System we are primarily concerned with five human needs:

- the need for Economic Security
- the need to Control
- the need for Recognition
- the need for Personal Self-worth
- the need to Belong

An understanding of human needs is the third principle of the OMS and an integral part of the Circle of Reference. Understanding human needs is the key to working effectively with others.

The relationship between individual human needs and individual performance objectives is a significant one. As we have seen, in the Open Management System one not only attempts to identify the maximum need, but also tries to satisfy it in a positive way—often by providing opportunities in which the need can be channeled and transformed into a strength. Thus, the individual's self-image is also strengthened and enhanced.

When a performance objective is clearly established, the channel through which need satisfaction can be accomplished also becomes apparent. But the performance objective must be determined first; only then does one know how to go about providing need satisfaction and enhancing the self-image.

The third step in the MWP is to develop and implement an action plan. This plan is composed of two parts: a description of what is to be done, and an indication of how often this action is to be taken. While this may at first appear to be self-evident, the frequency of an action often determines its effectiveness. (This last will be discussed in detail in the chapter dealing with the various types of action plans.)

The action plan is essential to the practical application of the principles of OMS. Without it, OMS is only a theory.

One of the difficulties inherent in any action plan is that the plan might be selected before the objective has been defined. Often, the pressure on managers and employees is so great that people take action—any action—before they have any very good idea of what it is they wish to accomplish.

So the action plan is the last step in the MWP, not because it is any less important than the others, but because in order to develop and implement the *right* action it is necessary first to have a performance objective clearly in mind, and to identify the maximum human need which must be satisfied in order to accomplish that objective.

Every plan requires follow-up. Without follow-up one has no way of knowing whether he has properly defined the objective, identified the maximum human need, and selected an appropriate action plan. The time for follow-up obviously varies with the situation. In all cases, however, some form of follow-up is essential.

A Module for Working with People is illustrated in Figure 21 on page 139. The various elements will be discussed in more detail in subsequent chapters.

A Stradivarius violin is only carved wood with strings attached until it is played by a skilled musician. The same is true of the MWP. Until it is put into practice, it has little value.

One more thing: While the Module is shown in graphic form, it is not always necessary to actually duplicate it on paper. What *is* important is that the three-step approach be kept firmly in mind.

THE MODULE
FOR WORKING WITH PEOPLE

NAME
_____ JOB
TITLE _____
1. The Performance Objective(s)

2. Human Need Identification

Human Needs	Observed Range		
	Minimum	Average	Maximum
Need for Economic Security	☐	☐	☐
Need to Control	☐	☐	☐
Need for Recognition	☐	☐	☐
Need for Personal Self-worth	☐	☐	☐
Need to Belong	☐	☐	☐

3. Action Plan
   a. What to do:

   b. How often?

Review Date_____
Follow-up Date_____

Figure 21

11. GUIDELINES FOR DETERMINING PERFORMANCE OBJECTIVES

How to Develop Individual
Performance Objectives

MUCH HAS has been written about objectives, but objectives themselves are difficult to discuss—mainly because it is rarely clear what or who the objectives are *for*. The term "objectives" can refer to any number of things: objectives for a company, objectives for a department, a group, a manager, an individual employee, or for oneself.

For our purposes an objective is what one person has in mind when working with another person in a business environment, and includes the relationships of managers and employees—laterally and up and down the organizational environment.

So, in OMS an objective involves a one-to-one relationship between any two people in the organization and refers to whatever *should* be done that is not being done at present. There are two implications here: First, that the person setting the performance objective for the other person must know where that other person stands now in relation to the objective; second, that the person setting the performance objective must know how and in what way the other person's performance must be modified.

Let's consider someone just setting out on a trip to Chicago. In order to advise him of the best way to get there, one would have to know the point from which he is starting. Obviously, if he is starting from New York he would take one route; from San Francisco he would take another. In either case, the objective is the same—to get to Chicago—but the routes are quite different. In a similar way, if it is known that a person is beginning a journey from New York, before one could advise him on a route one would also have to know his destination.

Often people talk about "goals" and "objectives." During the course of our research, we have noted that the terms are used interchangeably—although some try to differentiate between short-term goals and long-term objectives, or vice versa. In the Open Management System we stay with the term "objectives," and they may be either short- or long-term.

As previously pointed out, objectives are difficult to describe, often because they are so vague and general. But in the Open Management System the preparation of objectives is made easier by defining objectives in terms of performance.

This is a matter of asking oneself what one wishes to accomplish with another person. A clear answer to this question is the first element of the Module for Working with People. By stating a performance objective—what it is that one wishes to accomplish by working with another person—managers and employees are both in a better position to reach the designated performance objective through the individual's maximum human need. The action plan becomes meaningful only after the performance objective has been stated and the maximum human need understood.

In OMS, determining a performance objective is a personal thing. It is a decision made solely by the individual determining the objective. Whether the other person shares the objective—or how he shares the objective—is not a part of the determination. It *is* a part of the action plan. The third element of the Module, the action plan, is sometimes erroneously substituted for a performance objective, often at times when the pressure to do something is very great. Under such circumstances, one is tempted to omit a performance objective and simply act—do something to relieve pressure.

We urge you always to determine a performance objective. It will help

1. to select the best action plan—the one that can contribute most toward accomplishing the objective.

2. to avoid action plans that might not contribute toward the accomplishment of the objective.

3. to determine whether the *real* problem is clearly understood.

4. to save time in the long run.

5. to provide personal satisfaction for accomplishments.

In the OMS Module approach, the objective and the action plan are separated by the human needs of the person involved. Each part of the Module is distinct. This three-step method ties all the elements together in a meaningful way.

A good performance objective answers the question "What do I want the other person to do?" or "What do I want done differently from the way it is being done now?"

Preparation of a good performance objective is just as important as the plan to implement it. Albert Einstein once said that "The mere formulation of a problem is far more essential than its solution." The implication, of course, is: Asking the right question is the most important element in resolving any performance problem; or, as John Dewey stressed, a problem is half solved when it is properly stated.

Preparing performance objectives is a skill that can be developed and improved upon. While ability may vary, proficiency always increases through practice. It's the same as learning to play the piano or tennis. One must first learn the fundamental elements—after that, most of one's time is spent in practicing. But practice alone is not enough; it must be the proper kind of practice.

Often, in preparing a performance objective time

is wasted because the objective is poorly stated or incomplete or the *real* objective has not been ascertained.

An objective is an intent, and a performance objective is a description of what we want someone else to do. Thus, a performance objective properly indicates a desire for some sort of change on the part of another person. In setting a performance objective, we are not concerned with whether or not the person involved can do what we want him to do, or why he isn't doing it now, or whether he used to do it well but doesn't any more, or any other similar considerations. These are all very proper questions to ask, but not now, while preparing the objective. They can and should be asked later, when one is determining the action plan through which the performance objective will be accomplished.

A performance objective often requires a certain amount of time to accomplish. But unless the performance objective is clear in the mind of the person stating it, there is no way to evaluate or measure partial performance or partial accomplishment of the objective.

A well-written performance objective describes where one wishes to go, not how to get there. The objective must be written so that the writer can indeed know if the other person can accomplish or has accomplished what has been specified. Thus, it is necessary to be able to observe and measure results, because it is only through the actions of the other person that one can tell if the objective has been reached.

The question often arises: How detailed should a performance objective be? The question is similar to the one about how long a piece of string should be (long enough to do the job).

A good performance objective is detailed insofar as the writer's intent is clear to himself. In some cases very few words are needed; in others several sentences may be required. While a brief, specific statement often is less ambiguous than a longer one, there is no rule here, and the amount of detail included in the performance objective is best left to the discretion of the writer.

Sometimes—though not always—a performance objective includes a criterion of how well a thing is to be done. Once again, this is to be determined by the person writing the performance objective. For instance, to increase output by 6 percent is a performance objective, and it is implied that the greater production output will meet accepted standards. However, if there is some question about what these standards are, then they should be specified. If the performance objective is one according to which an individual is to do a thing better than he does it presently, the stating of criteria may be very important (time, cost, speed, quality, etc.)

A performance objective always states what *should* be done, rather than how to do it. If there are several things that should be done, each must be stated as a separate performance objective. When several unrelated objectives are combined, it is difficult to determine an effective action plan. It is also next to impossible to observe and measure the individual's performance and relate it to a particular objective if multiple unrelated objectives are combined.

One might liken a multiple performance objective to starting on a trip for three or four or more places at the same time. Eventually one might reach all destinations, but consecutively, certainly not simultaneously.

When several performance objectives are combined, ambiguity results. Often, people who are unsure of just what they wish to do write multiple objectives. Having one specific concise objective for each thing to be done helps to keep things clear.

In short, then, performance objectives should be:

1. measurable or observable
2. realistic and obtainable
3. specific
4. individual
5. written

The first guideline, that performance objectives be observable and measurable, insures that one can determine whether or not the subsequent action plan has been successful. Measurable objectives would include those that specify dates, times, percentages, numbers, dollars, etc. The following examples illustrate performance objectives that are measurable:

That Roger increase his output by 12 percent over last year's output within the next six months.

That Jim reduce sales expenses by 8 percent within twelve months without losing market position.

That Alice be late no more than three times within the next three months.

That customer complaints about Nancy be reduced by 6 percent in the next eight weeks.

That Edward approve without changes seven letters more per week.

That Raymond approve expense accounts within three days.

That Doris maintain a reserve of 10 percent of office forms within the next month.

Such objectives are easy to measure, because they specify numbers, percentages, and dates. Whenever possible, a performance objective should be measurable. Otherwise, one has no very good way of ascertaining whether it has been accomplished.

While the sample performance objectives might have been stated somewhat differently by another person, the major point is that the writer know in his own mind exactly what he wishes to have done. This implies that the writer also knows how things stand now in relation to the performance objective. For example, the writer must be aware of Roger's present performance before he can set a performance objective for the next six months. This is true for all performance objectives.

Of course, in dealing with people it is not always possible to assign measurable variables; often it may be necessary to state the objective in a way that cannot be precisely measured but must instead be observed.

While it is true that there are ways to assign numerical values for almost any situation, a numerical measurement may not be the proper criterion of an individual's performance. For example, it is easy to measure the number of A's and F's a particular teacher hands out to his students, and if the objective is to determine the number of A's and F's handed out, one simply counts them. If, however, the objective is to determine the teacher's effectiveness in creating a desire to learn, some other criteria are required—such as the attitude of the students, their attentiveness, their willingness to participate, and so forth. These criteria are not easily measured, but they can be observed.

Observations can be made by anyone who is aware

of the criteria. Consider an observation as to whether a particular person is walking fast or slow. We can say that he is walking fast, and in general our meaning will be understood. In a similar manner in the business environment, judgments regarding a person's performance can be made and used.

For example, it would certainly be difficult to assign a numerical value when the objective is to improve morale in a certain office. But it would be quite apparent to a perceptive observer that morale had or had not improved. (While it is true that occasionally improved morale can be related to increased production, one should remember that improvement in morale just as often does not increase production. Improved morale and increased production are two quite separate objectives.)

Another example of how performance objectives can be observed might concern an employee in a department that has less-than-harmonious relationships with another department in the company. Suppose that in this situation the trouble between the two departments is caused by one manager's relationship with the other department's manager. The employee might state as his performance objective that his manager improve interdepartmental relations. The result certainly would be observable.

When it is possible to measure the objective, this should be done. When the objective cannot be measured, the writer must learn to depend for an evaluation on what he observes and how he feels about it.

The second OMS guideline for setting performance objectives is that the objective be realistic or observable *from the other person's point of view*. One of the pitfalls in setting performance objectives is that the objectives are unrealistic.

For instance, consider a manager who has an employee who comes to work between thirty and forty minutes late every single day. The manager wants this employee to come to work on time. As a perceptive manager, he knows that it might be too much to expect that the employee completely change his habits within just a few days. While this could be a feasible long-range objective, it would be unrealistic as a short-range one.

In general, then, objectives should be attainable with a reasonable expenditure of effort. If great effort is required at any one time, the individual may be discouraged from even trying. People need to feel that they are making progress toward an objective. If the performance objective is set so high as to be practically unattainable, then often, in order to avoid the pain of frustration and failure, no attempt will even be launched to try to achieve it.

A manager may want an employee to improve his relations with fellow employees, be more punctual in posting accounts, speed up his correspondence, and avoid safety violations. But if all these things are stated at one time, the manager will be setting unrealistic performance objectives; there simply are too many of them. In the same way, an employee may wish to have his manager accept more of his suggestions for improving efficiency in the section. If the boss presently does not accept any of his suggestions, it would be unrealistic to expect him to do a complete turnaround and accept all the employee's suggestions. A more feasible objective would be to have a single suggestion accepted.

The third guideline for setting performance objectives concerns specificity. Even brilliant managers often fail to be specific enough. Yet failure to be specific is a most serious pitfall in preparing objectives. When a performance objective is vague, it is difficult to carry through with an action plan. When a performance objective is not specific, it is next to impossible to measure or observe, and probably will also be unrealistic. In general, avoid writing objectives that contain ambiguous statements or generalizations such as "Do a better job," "Increase output," "Stop complaining," "Work harder," "Be more understanding."

To illustrate why this is important, let's consider a manager whose department was consistently criticized for its uncooperative attitude. His performance objective for his employees was that they become "more cooperative." While the manager may have had some understanding of what he wished to have done, the objective was so vague that no one did anything.

Another example concerns an employee whose supervisor complained regularly about the poor quality of work turned out by the group. The employee wanted the supervisor to be more understanding of the situation and aware of the problems that made the low-quality work inevitable. Little progress was made, because the objective was not specific.

The fourth guideline for setting performance objectives has to do with focusing on an individual.

There are—and should be—corporate objectives, divisional objectives, departmental objectives, and so forth. But in the Open Management System, we must emphasize again, we are concerned with performance objectives set by one person for another. This is not to say that individual performance objectives had not best be congruent with corporate objectives. They usually should be and are. However, if they are to be meaningful to a particular person and his job, they should be written with that particular person in mind. A one-to-one relationship must be set up between the person writing the objective and the person for whom the objective is being written. Such relationships are crucial to implementing the Open Management System. They are the key to making it work.

A departmental objective might be to increase output by 14 percent within the next twelve months. To do this, an individual objective for an employee within the department might be to reduce by fifteen minutes a day the time wasted socializing with other employees. The departmental goal and the individual goal are different but congruent.

The fifth guideline for setting a performance objective is that it be stated on paper.

Actually putting an objective down on paper is the best way to insure that it will be measurable or observable, realistic or obtainable, specific, and focused on an individual. In its written form, the objective is easily evaluated in terms of meeting these criteria. Performance objectives that can't be stated in writing exist only as fuzzy concepts—and if the concept is vague and undefined, it is impossible to develop an action plan that works. One can compare it to going on a trip without knowing where one is headed: If you don't know where you want to go, any old road will do.

THE MANAGER'S VIEWPOINT

In order to be effective, a manager must know where he is going. This means having a performance objective for each employee. In this way, within a specific period of time he will know if he is moving closer to his own objective. The following examples illustrate the importance of preparing good performance objectives.

The Case of the Head Clerk

Al Chamberlain was operations manager of the Carlton Manufacturing Company. Recently he appointed Susan Dorsey as office supervisor. One of Miss Dorsey's duties was to handle requisitions for the purchase of office supplies and miscellaneous materials. Since taking over this job, she had become very concerned about the increased expenditure of money for office supplies. She spent many hours checking and rechecking invoices against the petty-cash balance. She guarded the order book as though it were her personal property, and required a detailed explanation for every proposed requisition.

Al noted that Susan spent too much time on what was, after all, only a minor part of her job. Also, other people's time was being wasted in arguing with Susan about when she would get the materials they needed, and complaining about the poor quality of some of the low-priced materials she kept ordering. Morale among the employees in the office seemed to be declining.

Al was a perceptive man who understood the

principles of the Open Management System. He knew that the first step in applying OMS principles in this situation was to develop a performance objective for Susan Dorsey. As Al reviewed the situation in his mind, he realized that he might have to set several performance objectives for her. But he decided to begin by developing one performance objective at this time, and wrote it up as follows:

"To have Susan approve 25 percent more requisitions for office supplies without requiring detailed explanations of how the material is to be used. This is to be accomplished within the next thirty days."

Let's analyze the objective to see if it is in accordance with OMS guidelines for good performance objectives.

The first guideline is that the objective be measurable or observable. Al stated that he wished the change in Susan's performance to be accomplished within thirty days. He also indicated a 25 percent improvement over what she had been doing. Thus, it was quite easy for Al to determine if the performance objective had been achieved.

The second guideline is that the objective be realistic. A certain amount of judgment on the part of the person setting the objective is required here. In the long run, Al probably would have liked Susan to approve all or nearly all requisitions in this manner. However, he felt that it would have been unrealistic to expect Susan to change completely all at once. Asking a person to do more than is possible at any one time is a mistake—and one that is often made. The longest journey begins with a single step, and if one is to get there at all it is more important to get started in the right direction than to worry about the length of the journey.

The third guideline for performance objectives is that the objective be specific. Al set a performance objective of 25 percent within thirty days, which met this requirement. Numbers, percentages, dates, and the like are helpful in making performance objectives specific.

The fourth guideline is that it focus on an individual. Al saw that a number of other persons might be affected by this situation, but Susan was most responsible for the dissatisfaction in the department, and so he wrote the objective for her.

The fifth guideline for setting performance objectives is to write it down, and this, of course, he did.

The time spent in setting a good performance objective will be well worthwhile. Not only will it indicate the best action plan, it will also help satisfy maximum human needs.

What's Going On?

Bill Snyder was in the Credit Card Department of the Central States Petroleum Co. He was a young man, and very interested in getting ahead in the company. Bill's department was a highly specialized one. Each of the employees in the Credit Department had his own specific responsibilities. Although they conferred from time to time on some matters, it usually was not necessary for Bill to attend these meetings. Nevertheless, Bill went out of his way to appear at them.

Some of the meetings lasted for several hours.

Occasionally a meeting degenerated into a story-telling session. When this happened, Bill was quick to come up with various anecdotes of his own. This had happened recently: Bill had told a few stories and then proceeded to become involved in the main discussion later on, as the meeting progressed.

Very often the meetings were taken up with matters of no concern to Bill. However, he seemed anxious to get involved anyway. Some of the other men in the department resented Bill's constant presence and were beginning to grumble about the situation. Burke Benson, the manager of the Credit Card Department, sensed that a rather serious problem was developing, and wondered what he could do to keep things running smoothly.

Burke decided that his performance objective would be to have Bill stay out of any meeting to which he had not been invited.

Obviously, this would be a readily observable objective: Bill either would or would not attend meetings to which he had not been invited. Thus, Burke's performance objective was in accordance with the first guideline.

The second guideline is that the performance objective be realistic. Burke's objective probably was not realistic. Keeping Bill away from all meetings might have been too much to ask at the beginning.

The third guideline, specificity, also was not met by Burke's objective, since it was somewhat vague as to which meetings were involved, what was meant by an invitation, and when this was to take place.

Burke's performance objective *was* individual, and was in accordance with the fourth guideline, but it was not written down, since Burke decided to simply tell

Bill about it. (Also, the telling was part of Burke's action plan, rather than a part of his performance objective.)

The Case of the Impressive Employee

Reg Pritchard was an assistant supervisor in the Data Processing department. Reg was only recently appointed to his current job, and according to his boss had a lot of potential ability. As he said, "Once Reg understands the traditions of our business, he'll be okay."

Reg wore high-fashion clothes, drove a new convertible, and often went to lunch at expensive restaurants. It was said that at one of the company's weekly staff meetings Reg's knowledge of the Data Processing department's activities made quite an impression on some of the older managers.

Harry Stoner, Reg's boss and the Data Processing department's supervisor, recently became concerned about Reg's behavior. Reg often just seemed to sit and stare into space. On one occasion it was reported that Reg seemed interested only in trying to impress one of the company's customers with his knowledge. Reg was overheard saying to a customer that he was administration manager—a job classification that didn't exist.

Since Reg had potential and a good knowledge of the business, but didn't do too much work, Harry wanted to find ways to motivate Reg to do more work.

Harry decided that his performance objective for Reg would be related to one of Reg's prime responsibilities, which was to keep up on proposed changes in customer data-processing procedures and then implement these changes as quickly as possible. Harry saw that

Reg had been falling behind in this assignment, and decided to make this a part of his performance objective. Harry wrote his performance objective as follows:

"To have Reg contact five additional customers each week—starting at once—to insure that the present procedures are meeting their needs and to determine if any changes are being planned."

Let's analyze the objective to see if it meets the guidelines of the Open Management System.

The first guideline, remember, is that the objective be measurable or observable. Harry stated that he wanted Reg to contact five additional customers each week—something that was easily measured or observed.

The second guideline for a good performance objective is that it be realistic or obtainable. This, of course, is a subjective matter; decision as to what is realistic or obtainable must be made in the mind of the person writing the objective. In doing so, it is necessary to keep the other's viewpoint in mind; if the objective is seen as being unattainable, chances are no serious effort will be made to achieve it. Harry's objective, to have Reg make five customer calls per week, was, he felt, a realistic one for Reg to accomplish.

The third guideline is that the performance objective be specific. Harry *had* been specific by stressing a particular activity that was included in Reg's job responsibilities. This is the way it should be. Remember: Generalizations, such as "doing a better job" and "working harder," are too vague to be meaningful.

The fourth guideline for setting performance objectives is that it focus on an individual. Harry recognized that he was writing a performance objective for

Reg. (At the same time, he might have also been setting performance objectives for others in the department, as well as departmental objectives, which he might later have written down separately.)

The fifth guideline for setting performance objectives is to write it down. Harry did this. One obvious benefit of writing an objective is that one can refer back to it to see if the objective has been concisely and clearly stated. A written objective is also more concrete, and serves as a guide in developing a positive action plan.

Writing performance objectives that are in keeping with the Open Management System guidelines requires concentrated attention to the problem. Otherwise, the writer of the objective and the person for whom it is written will both have little basis for understanding what is to be done.

THE EMPLOYEE'S VIEWPOINT

In order to work effectively with a manager, an employee needs to know what he seeks to accomplish. For this one must have a performance objective for the manager. Thus, within a specific period of time one can know if the objective is being met.

Harold Nichols, a customer-claims clerk, wanted to obtain from his boss, Jim Higgins, approval to authorize claims up to fifty dollars. Harold had to go to Jim for approval of every customer claim regardless of the amount involved. Harold felt that he had sufficient experience to be able to make certain decisions on his own. He also knew that if he received Jim's permission to authorize claims up to fifty dollars, Jim would have more time for other tasks. Harold knew that if Jim accepted his suggestion, customer-claim settlements would be speeded up. So, as an employee familiar with the Open Management System, Harold decided to write a performance objective for Jim as follows:

"To have Jim delegate the authority to approve customer claims up to fifty dollars within the next thirty days."

Let's analyze this performance objective to see if it was in accordance with the guidelines of the Open Management System.

The first guideline is that the performance objective be measurable or observable. Harold's objective was easy to measure and observe.

The second guideline is that the performance objective be realistic. Jim did spend a considerable part of his time reviewing and approving Harold's recommendations. His acceptance of Harold's suggestion would have speeded up claims approvals and contributed to better customer relations. It could easily have been implemented in the thirty-day period.

The third guideline for performance objectives is that it be specific. By specifying *all* customer claims up to fifty dollars, Harold's objective met this requirement. Claims over fifty dollars would still require Jim's approval.

The fourth guideline for preparing performance objectives is that it be individual. Harold saw the situation from Jim's point of view and considered Jim's individual role in this activity.

The fifth guideline for preparing performance objectives is that it be written down, and Harold did this. So

Harold's written performance objective met all the OMS criteria.

The Case of the Disgruntled Department

Kevin Dickens was manager of the Appraisal Department of the Westbrook Bank, where he had worked for sixteen years. During his career he had held various jobs, beginning as a teller and working his way up to his current position. Kevin had been the manager of the Appraisal Department for nine years.

Kevin had a thorough knowledge of the business of his department, and believed in abiding by company policy no matter what his personal opinions might be. Kevin had a high rate of turnover in his department.

Kevin really felt that the new, less-experienced appraisers had too many unconventional ways of doing their jobs. He said more than once, "These young upstarts think they know better ways to do their jobs than the way I've been telling them to do it. Believe me, I know my business, and when these guys finally start doing things my way, then they'll see I'm right."

Henry Darton, one of the best appraisers in Kevin's group, had a program to eliminate some of the problems in the Appraisal Department. He wondered how to get Kevin to adopt the program.

In reviewing the situation, Henry decided to point out to Kevin the many problems that existed in his department. While dong so, Henry told Kevin that unless some of these difficulties were taken care of, the only alternative would be for him to quit. Some time passed since the interview between them, and nothing was done.

In analyzing Henry's performance objective, we

can see that any changes Kevin might have brought about would have been readily observable. Thus, the first guideline for good performance objectives was satisfied.

The second guideline is that the performance objective be realistic or obtainable. The performance objective *was* realistic—from Henry's point of view. One must always remember that objectives should be written with the *other* person's viewpoint in mind. Henry's was not. For Kevin to bring about all the procedural changes Henry wanted him to make, all at once, was an unrealistic expectation.

A better approach would have been to suggest one particular change that could have been implemented immediately and without posing a threat to Kevin. Also, Henry might have offered assistance to Kevin in a positive way to help him make this particular change.

Henry, in fact, made a poor choice of a performance objective for Kevin, because it was impractical and unrealistic; this is always apt to be the case when the other person's viewpoint is not considered.

The third guideline, that of aiming for specificity, was satisfied by Henry's statement that he would quit. Unfortunately, though, the statement has to do with Henry, not Kevin.

The fourth guideline for a good performance objective is that it must be individual. As we have seen, Henry developed the objective for himself, and it therefore applied to the wrong person. Henry had himself in mind, especially when he said he would quit if things were not changed. If Henry had considered Kevin's individual performance objective, both men might have been winners.

The fifth guideline for a good performance objective is that it be written. Henry did not put his objective down on paper, but talked with Kevin instead. As we have pointed out, implementation of the performance objective is a part of the action plan, and comes later. So Henry's action—talking to Kevin—was premature.

The Barrington Duplex

Alice Freeman was a real-estate saleswoman in the city of Oakdale. She had been working with Doug Hollenbeck, who seemed to be interested in buying the Barrington duplex.

Alice consistently emphasized its modern architecture, its proximity to golf clubs and excellent schools. In spite of all these advantages, Doug remained hesitant about making a final commitment.

Doug was fifty-six years old, drove a six-year-old automobile, dressed very conservatively, and had inquired several times about the cost/return ratio of the building. He had also asked about taxes, interest rates, and monthly payments for various terms.

During her last meeting with Doug, Alice emphasized the prime location of the property and its resale value. She also stressed the excellent cost/return ratio. Doug again expressed interest in the property, but still did not agree to purchase. Alice wondered what she should do next.

Alice knew that of all the duplexes available in the area, the Barrington duplex would be the most suitable for Doug. Because she was familiar with the Open Management System, Alice decided to develop a performance objective for Doug. It was written as follows:

"To have Doug buy the Barrington duplex during the next ten days and for a price within the range established by the seller."

Let's analyze her performance objective to see if it was in accordance with OMS guidelines.

As for its being measurable or observable, Alice would certainly have known whether her performance objective had been achieved, simply by Doug's decision to buy—or not to buy—the Barrington duplex within the established price range and time specified.

The second guideline is that the performance objective be realistic, which must be determined by the person setting the performance objective. Alice knew that Doug was able to buy the Barrington duplex and that it was well suited to his needs, and so to her the objective did indeed seem reasonable.

The third guideline for a performance objective is that it be specific. Based on her knowledge of the property and her perceptive observation of Doug, Alice had decided that this particular duplex was well suited to him.

The fourth guideline is that the performance objective be realistic, which must be determined by the many prospective buyers, she considered Doug as an individual buyer with unique requirements, and wrote her performance objective accordingly.

The fifth guideline for preparing a performance objective is that it be written, and this Alice did. A written objective served as reminder to Alice of exactly what she was trying to do.

Setting a performance objective is a personal thing. It involves a relationship between two persons, in which one person has something specific in mind which he wishes the other person to do. The objective is determined by the person setting it and accomplished through the actions of the second person. Anything beyond this is not properly a part of the performance objective.

There are two essential elements in determining a performance objective: Where one is now in a relationship with the other person, and where one would like to be at some future time. As in going on a journey, one must know the starting point and where one wishes to end up.

In the OMS the objective must be clear in the mind of the person determining it. (Once again we emphasize that the performance objective and its implementation are two separate steps.) But what if one isn't sure about what the other person should do? When this is the case, and it often is, one simply cannot write a performance objective. However, it frequently happens that the attempt to write an objective clarifies the issue. Certainly, with practice one develops the ability to think in terms of objectives, and the task becomes easier.

What about selecting the wrong performance objective? This is always a possibility. But, continuing the analogy of the person going on a trip, if that person decided to go from New York to Chicago, he might soon realize that Chicago is the wrong objective and that he should go to St. Louis instead. This realization may come before he gets to Chicago, or not until after he arrived. Since the objective was set by the individual, it can be changed by the individual, and this should be done as soon as an error is perceived.

Setting a performance objective is not the same as

implementing it. Too often, people seek to do something before they know what must be done. The merging of the two—setting an objective and implementing it—is the greatest pitfall confronting those who try to set objectives. One way to get around this difficulty is through the concept of satisfying human needs.

In our next chapter the relationship between the performance objective and human needs will be shown.

12. HOW TO IDENTIFY HUMAN NEEDS

THE SECOND element of the Module for Working with People is human need identification. Once again, the human needs under consideration here are the same ones that have been discussed in previous chapters.

As you recall, the third principle of OMS is to understand and satisfy individual human needs (need for economic security, need to control, need for recognition, need for feelings of personal self-worth, need to belong). The third element of the Circle of Reference also concerns individual human needs.

Obviously, all sensible human actions are directed

toward the satisfaction of human needs. If those needs can be satisfied on the job, it follows that the job will bring a sense of fulfillment. When needs can be satisfied only off the job, then the job will be boring and/or frustrating.

Although we defined these human needs as being separate and distinct, in actuality they are interwoven within each individual personality.

The perceptive observer notes the words and actions of another person and from these words and actions is able to identify that person's maximum human need. We are concerned with making this identification so that it will be possible to create the environment in which the need and the person can be satisfied.

Many people have two maximum needs. Some have only one. Others have as many as three. A few have no very strong needs; their greatest need would be considered as no more compelling than average.

In some situations a human need will change from maximum to average, even minimum, but most often a maximum need will continue to be maximum. Barring drastic changes of circumstances or in the environment, needs are in a state of equilibrium and stay at the same level of intensity.

Examples of a drastic change in circumstances include a promotion, failure to get a promotion, a forced transfer to another location. Although a change in the maximum human need might be only temporary, the perceptive observer will recognize the change and seek to satisfy whatever need is *currently* maximum. In the ordinary day-to-day situation confronting managers and employees, the one or two maximum human needs will remain reasonably constant.

Anyone can learn the techniques for identifying maximum human needs. One simply becomes attentive to the pattern and the symbols with which each person surrounds himself. By looking and listening to what is going on, it is possible to understand the true meaning of what we see and hear. Ordinarily we know quite a lot about other people, and the efforts of the perceptive observer are bent toward weaving together bits and pieces of information into meaningful patterns. The less-perceptive person overlooks or rejects or ignores these little bits of information which, if understood, could provide the clues by which to recognize maximum human needs. When one wants to become a better golfer, it is not enough simply to read books about how successful golfers get that way. One must also practice. If one wishes to become a keen observer, it is necessary to practice being perceptive; learning how is 90 percent attitude and 10 percent skill. You *can* do it. In fact, you now *do* do it, in any important relationship in which you get along with another person (spouse, friend, etc.).

As we've said before, OMS supplies techniques for understanding, identifying, and satisfying a person's maximum human needs. The Module for Working with People is a tool to help both managers and employees practice these concepts on the job every day. The approach suggested by the Module enables you to span the gap between good theory and good practice.

The MWP is a three-step plan. Step #1, discussed in the previous chapter, is to set a performance objective. Step #2 is concerned with identifying human needs.

The relationshop between a performance objective and the individual's maximum human need should be kept in mind. Once the objective has been decided upon, the perceptive observer sets about identifying the maximum human need of the person for whom the objective was written.

In identifying an individual's maximum human need, it is important to *avoid making a judgment.* This is especially true when the individual's maximum human need is very different from one's own. For instance, when an individual's maximum human need is for economic security while one's own need for economic security is minimum, there is a tendency to make a judgment of the other person's need as "good" or "bad." By being aware of everybody's natural tendency to evaluate (or judge) the needs of others, one can develop an ability to identify needs objectively.

One must also keep in mind the first principle of OMS: to see a situation from the other person's point of view. This includes seeing the individual need from the other person's point of view—which also helps in avoiding a judgment regarding the need.

While the second principle of OMS is to identify and build on individual strengths, there is a tendency to see another's maximum need as a weakness and something that must be overcome. But in OMS we try to view maximum needs as strengths, and to recognize that a reinforcement of the need will be well received. Any effort to change or overcome the maximum need will result in frustration.

All people seek to satisfy their particular maximum human needs. Satisfaction can be achieved in either positive or negative ways. A child may have a maximum human need for recognition. To satisfy this need, he may wish to show his father something he made during the day. If, because of a hectic day at work, the father is tired and wants to relax for a while on arriving home, he may dismiss the child abruptly with something such as "I'll play with you later. Don't bother me now." The child's need for recognition remains unsatisfied. He may then go to his mother and try to get her attention in some way. But if she's busy preparing dinner or involved in other activities, she too may dismiss the child, and the need for recognition remains unsatisfied.

The result? The child goes to another room and makes loud noises or turns the TV volume way up. In response to the noise, both the father and mother quickly come to see what has happened. Result? The child gets the recognition he desires, and the need is satisfied, but in a negative way. How much better if the need could have been satisfied in a positive way so all could have benefited!

Needs can be satisfied in positive and negative ways in a business environment, too.

Dorothy, who frequently was late for work, and didn't bother to call to say she would be late, disrupted the office routine. Dorothy had a strong need for recognition which was not satisfied in her work. After repeated warnings and verbal reprimands, her supervisor finally decided to punish Dorothy by giving her three days off without pay. In a quiet voice, the supervisor informed Dorothy of his decision. Much to his surprise, she responded, in a loud voice, "Great! Why not make it five days so I can go skiing?"

Dorothy satisfied her need for recognition by being late, and got further satisfaction through the reprimands she received from her supervisor and then by shouting loudly (for all to hear) about her disciplinary layoff. Her need was satisfied, but in a negative way.

In both examples, the maximum human need of the individual was satisfied negatively. But if the parents of the young child had responded to his need and provided an opportunity for the need to be satisfied positively, the child would not have found it necessary to create a commotion. If Dorothy's supervisor had been a perceptive observer, he would have seen Dorothy's lateness as a symbol of her need for recognition, and would have taken steps to satisfy the need in a positive way (which might also have solved the late-arrival problem).

When it comes to satisfying human needs, age makes no difference. All people, young and old, have human needs, and these *must* be satisfied. Human needs are part of the individual and exist for that individual both on and off the job.

In the work environment, when a manager creates conditions that satisfy his employees' maximum human needs he strengthens his whole group or department. When an employee satisfies his manager's maximum human need, the group or department is also strengthened. Since both managers and employees are better off when their needs are satisfied, it is mutually beneficial to apply OMS principles both ways. Win-win situations are the result.

While creating a need-satisfying environment is important, it is also important to avoid conditions which may threaten need satisfaction. A person with a maximum need to belong wishes to be a part of the group and feels threatened if he senses that he may be singled out for any reason. A person with a strong need for economic security may feel threatened if his job requires him to spend his own money to entertain a client. It is important to identify maximum human needs in order to avoid situations and conditions that threaten them.

All managers and employees might ask themselves these questions:

In what ways can I satisfy the maximum human needs of others?

In what ways can I avoid threatening their maximum human needs?

Another important reason for identifying maximum human needs is that if and when an opportunity presents itself to satisfy another's human need, it should be the maximum need that gets the greatest response.

Human needs are identifiable through human symbols. People literally wear signs indicating what their maximum human needs are. Again, to identify these needs, one must pay attention, listen, and observe.

A person who works with several other people may want to be fair with each of them. In his efforts to be fair, he may feel that he must spend equal amounts of time with each. This is not necessarily true, simply because individual human needs vary. Some people may need lots of attention. Others do better on less or almost none. The difference is due to their particular human needs.

The Module for Working People can help the perceptive observer identify the range of human needs for any person. The range extends from minimum through average to maximum. It has already been pointed out that most people have two human needs that can properly be labeled maximum. But what about the others? If there is no basis for rating an individual's human needs, we suggest that the needs be considered minimum. Often, when one has more information about the individual, it is possible to re-rate particular needs as being either average or maximum.

The following examples illustrate how various maximum human needs can be satisfied on the job.

THE MANAGER'S VIEWPOINT

An Evening with Ray

Bob Hopkins was eastern-operations vice-president of Dalton Enterprises. He frequently entertained VIPs from customer organizations. This was an important part of his job, and the good relationships that he had cultivated with these customers were reflected in a substantial increase in their business with Dalton.

Ray Culwell was Bob's very capable administrative assistant. Bob traveled extensively, and sometimes a VIP would arrive unexpectedly when Bob was out of town. Then it was Ray's responsibility to act for Bob and entertain the customer for the evening.

Although Ray understood the importance of this assignment, he did not believe in spending more than was absolutely necessary. From Ray's point of view, this was money foolishly spent. Ray had a pleasant-enough personality and got along well with people, but he always managed to have dinner at inexpensive, out-of-the-way restaurants. These evenings usually ended early.

Bob recently received word from one of Dalton's sales districts that the last customer Ray entertained had been offended by his obvious efforts to economize, and the district sales office was upset.

Bob was familiar with OMS, and decided to apply its principles to the situation.

The first step in using the Module for Working with People, remember, is to write a performance objective for what one wants another to do. Keeping in mind the guidelines for writing performance objectives, Bob developed the following for Ray:

"To have Ray differentiate between money spent frivolously and money spent in a way that will increase sales for Dalton Enterprise. This should be done before my next trip."

Bob's written performance objective for Ray was both measurable *and* observable. It was also realistic, specific, and individual for Ray.

The second step was for Bob to identify Ray's maximum human needs. From what he already knew about Ray, and by observing the pattern of Ray's human symbols, Bob identified Ray's two maximum human needs as the need for economic security and the need for feelings of personal self-worth.

Bob knew that the performance objective he set for Ray could best be accomplished through the satisfaction of his maximum human needs. So, in developing an action plan Bob took whatever steps were necessary to satisfy Ray's human needs and at the same time avoid actions that might be construed as threatening. This meant that he did not make judgments or laugh at Ray's thriftiness.

It became easy for him to emphasize with Ray that he appreciated Ray's willingness to give up an occasional evening to substitute for the boss (thereby building up Ray's self-worth) and point out to Ray that he was spending company money for entertainment, not his own funds. Furthermore, he reminded Ray that the company had repeatedly received solid evidence that it could chalk up this entertainment money as an investment which demonstrably paid off.

The Duke Freeman Case

Duke Freeman was manager of the credit department of the Pacific Western Company. Most of the people in Duke's group appeared to be uncooperative and unmotivated. There was a high rate of turnover in the department. Duke was the first one in every morning, and the last to leave at night.

Al Martin was manager of the company's data-processing department. Al had been trying to convince Duke to cooperate in trying a new system using the data-processing forms which Al's department recently developed. Every time Al met with Duke he told him about the success other departments were having after converting to the new forms. At their last meeting, when Al brought this up, Duke told him, "When my department needs better forms, I'll design them."

Al knew that Duke required all his people to let him know whenever they left the office. He signed all outgoing letters, reviewed all incoming mail, and once severely reprimanded a clerk for using the company phone for a personal emergency.

Al Martin was familiar with the Open Management System, and decided to apply its principles to this situation.

First, he wrote a performance objective, stating what he wanted Duke to do:

"To have Duke accept two of the new data-processing forms for the Credit Department within thirty days."

Al's written performance objective for Duke was both measurable and observable. It was realistic because it limited Duke's acceptance to two forms, rather than all ten in the series. It was specific—numbers and times were indicated—and it was individual for Duke.

Next, Al identified Duke's maximum human need. From his knowledge of Duke and his observation of Duke's human symbols, Al recognized that Duke's strongest need was the need to control.

Al understood that the performance objective he set for Duke could best be accomplished through the satisfaction of Duke's maximum human need. In developing an action plan, Al kept this need in mind and tried to satisfy it—by getting Duke involved in the design, testing, and redesign of new forms, listening carefully to Duke's ideas, responding respectfully and enthusiastically to them, and making sure that others in the company heard about Duke's contributions.

The Case of Catherine and Louise

Peggy Winslow was supervisor of the Save-By-Mail (SBM) section of the Oakdale Bank. Recently the Save-By-Mail department fell behind in its work, and customers were complaining about delays. P. M. Collins, the branch manager, wrote a memo to Peggy asking her for suggestions on how to speed up the processing of SBM postings by 15 percent.

Of the clerks in the SBM section, Catherine and Louise were typical. Peggy observed that the rest of the

SBM section followed their lead in most matters. She knew the following about them.

CATHERINE	Human Symbols	LOUISE
forty-eight years old	*age*	fifty-one years old
married, husband employed	*family*	married, husband employed
two grown children		three grown children
eighteen years	*seniority*	thirteen years
large house with pool	*home*	comfortable
elegant taste, very stylish	*dress*	plain, undistinguished
purple sports car	*car*	six-year-old green sedan
president, Oakdale Garden Club	*hobbies*	sewing and crocheting
talks incessantly	*habits*	very quiet
large picture of herself hostessing a charity bazaar	*desk*	small picture of grandchild

Peggy planned to apply the principles of the OMS. She was familiar with the Module for Working with People, but since more than one employee was involved, she knew that a separate Module was required for each woman.

Her first step was to write separate performance objectives for Catherine and Louise. The section objective, as set by the manager, called for an increase in the processing of SBM postings by 15 percent. (A section objective needn't be the same for each of the section's employees—though it could be. In all instances, however, individual performance objectives should be congruent with section objectives.)

Peggy, keeping OMS guidelines in mind, wrote the following performance objectives:

"To have Catherine reduce her socializing in the office by thirty minutes a day and spend this time on SBM customer complaints. This is to be done within ten days."

"To have Louise assist in the training of the newer employees in this section, starting at once."

Peggy's written performance objectives for Catherine and Louise were quite different, but both were designed to help Peggy meet the objective for her entire section: to increase SBM postings by 15 percent.

Note that Catherine's performance objective was both measurable and observable, while Louise's was observable.

Both objectives were realistic, specific, and individual.

Peggy's second step was to identify each woman's maximum human needs. From what she knew of Catherine, and by observing her human symbols, Peggy identified Catherine's maximum need as one for recognition. In the same way, she identified Louise's maximum human need as the need for feelings of personal self-worth and economic security.

Peggy knew that the individual performance objectives that she set for Catherine and Louise could best be accomplished by creating conditions that satisfied their maximum human needs. In developing action plans for the two women, she took the steps necessary to satisfy their needs, and in this way was able to accomplish the overall objective of her section. Catherine would be able to get satisfaction for her need for recognition by talking with customers about SBM complaints instead of socializing in the office.

The Case of the Reassuring Employee

Elmer Graham was manager of the design-engineering department of Eastwood Electronics Company. Elmer had been with Eastwood for twelve years. His record was very good. About nine years ago Elmer had been persuaded to try a new capacitor design. Within a short time many of the capacitors had failed, and as a result Elmer had been not only embarrassed but also severely criticized by his boss, the vice-president of Engineering. Ever since, Elmer had made sure that all equipment he approved for use at Eastwood Electronics had previously been proved elsewhere.

Elmer always asked questions like "Where has this been tried before?" "Who else has used this?" He had been heard to comment that he preferred the old days, when "things were less complicated."

As a result of Elmer's cautious attitude, Eastwood had become a follower—way behind their competitors in many important areas.

Tom Duncan, a young engineer in the design department, worked directly for Elmer. Tom had been with Elmer for about six months. He was very creative, and during his short time in the department had contributed some interesting ideas for product modifications.

Recently Tom developed a new circuit design which utilized a special low-loss transformer. He believed the design could be used effectively in a number of Eastwood products. Tom also knew that Eastwood was very much interested in developing new business.

Tom understood why Elmer accepted no new ideas for product changes unless they had been proved elsewhere, and wondered how he could convince Elmer to accept his own idea.

Tom knew OMS principles, and decided to apply them to the present situation. Keeping in mind the guidelines for writing performance objectives, he wrote the following:

"To have Elmer approve, within six weeks, the installation of a prototype of the low-loss transformer circuit design in one of Eastwood's production models."

Tom's performance objective for Elmer was measurable and observable. Based on Eastwood's production schedules, it was realistic for Tom to expect Eastwood to be able to produce the prototype within the six-week limitation. The objective was specific—it called for a particular design change to be made in one product—and individual—it was written with Elmer in mind.

Step #2 was for Tom to identify Elmer's maximum human need. From his knowledge of Elmer and his observation of Elmer's human symbols, which indicated a desire for constant reassurance, Tom identified Elmer's maximum human need as the need for feelings of personal self-worth.

Tom then saw that the performance objective he had set for Elmer could best be accomplished by attempting to satisfy Elmer's maximum human need. His action plan included taking appropriate steps to reassure Elmer that the circuit design was reliable and would not be a source of embarrassment. In this way Elmer's feeling of personal security would be satisfied and his own self-image as a worthwhile person would be enhanced.

Pants Suits on Friday

Marcia Brackett was manager of Corporate Control and Planning for a large Midwestern company. She was a graduate of one of the best women's colleges, and had been with the company in various supervisory positions for twelve years. Marcia was well organized and meticulous in everything she did, and her clothes, though stylish, tended to be rather formal and conservative.

Marcia spoke of herself as being a "part of the management team." Often, before making a decision she consulted with one of the other department managers. She belonged to the Women's Professional Society and three other groups involved in corporate-planning work.

Carolyn Wynne was a research analyst in Marcia's department. She was young, and had been in Marcia's department for less than a year. Carolyn was a casual, relaxed person. She hung some very bright modern posters near her desk. Last month she came to work wearing an orange pants suit. When Marcia saw this, she called Carolyn into her office and explained pleasantly but firmly that it was her policy to have all employees in her department dress in a traditional manner.

Carolyn was familiar with OMS principles, and decided to apply them. As a first step, she wrote the following performance objective:

"To have Marcia approve the wearing of pants suits on Fridays by female employees who want to do so. This is to be accomplished within two weeks."

Carolyn's performance objective for Marcia was measurable and observable. It was realistic because Carolyn had observed that a number of other women managers in the company wore pants suits from time to time, and because, as a start, Carolyn was suggesting that the pants suits be allowed on Fridays only. It was specific in that a particular day and time were mentioned, and it was individual for Marcia.

Carolyn then went on to identify Marcia's maximum human need. From what she knew about Marcia and by noting Marcia's human symbols, Carolyn identified Marcia's maximum need as the need to belong.

Carolyn knew that the performance objective she had set for Marcia could best be accomplished through the satisfaction of her need to belong. Her action plan took this into account, and Carolyn tried hard to avoid saying or doing anything that Marcia might see as a threat to her sense of belonging. This meant that Carolyn emphasized how, by approving her request, Marcia's status as an up-to-date manager within her own group could be enhanced.

These examples illustrate the distinct relationship existing between a good performance objective and the individual's maximum human needs.

Once again we emphasize that it is only by satisfying these needs in a positive way that a win-win situation can be created.

Goethe once said, "Behavior is a mirror in which everyone shows his image." Take a look and see for yourself the maximum human needs of others—they are open and available for you to see.

13. HOW TO DEVISE THE ACTION PLAN

THE FINAL step of the Module for Working with People concerns ways to satisfy maximum human needs in a way that relates directly to the performance objective.

A seed grows by itself. The farmer doesn't really "grow" it. Yet the farmer determines whether or not the seed comes to harvest. He provides an environment for the seed to grow successfully. He also recognizes that different seeds require different environments, and accommodates each according to its needs. Largely because of his efforts, some seeds produce a great harvest, some seeds produce a minimum harvest, other seeds die and produce nothing.

In the Open Management System the role of managers and employees is similar to that of the farmer: Through their efforts, an environment for growth and development can be created. Managers, using the principles of OMS, can cultivate conditions that enable employees to achieve personal satisfaction on the job. And employees can use OMS principles to create conditions enabling managers to achieve on-the-job satisfaction.

The environment in which both managers and employees get optimum job satisfaction is also the environment that is most beneficial for the company. Thus, OMS is a collection of concepts through which win-win situations are created and all participants gain.

The win-win environment is the result of a good one-to-one relationship. In OMS, managers consider individual employees' needs, and, in the same way, employees consider individual mangers' needs. In fact, it would not be stretching a point to say that the application of the OMS principles can create a favorable environment for growth and personal satisfaction in *any* one-to-one relationship, including relationships with fellow employees, fellow managers, and customers.

Again, the action plan is the third and final element of the Module for Working with People. (In most interpersonal relationships people begin with the equivalent of an action plan.) In general, what one does is successful more often than unsuccessful. But the application of the OMS principles will contribute substantially to making actions more successful than ever before.

An effective action plan is characterized by a

number of criteria. It must always satisfy the maximum human need of the person for whom it is intended. It should be directed toward accomplishing the performance objective developed as the first element of the Module for Working with People. The action plan should also be the means by which the individual's maximum human need is satisfied.

Obviously, an action plan can create either a positive or a negative environment. In a negative environment, the individual's self-image is threatened and the maximum human need goes unsatisfied. Performance objectives may be vague or impossible to achieve. Or the immediate performance objective may be accomplished but result in future dissatisfaction. A negative environment produces a lose-lose situation.

For example, a manager can curtail an individual's creativity by informing him that his ideas are not wanted, or by mocking him in front of others. The manager accomplishes the immediate objective of discouraging unwanted employee participation, but the long-range effect of this kind of approach is sure to be negative.

An employee can contribute to a negative environment for his boss by embarrassing him behind his back, or even publicly. This may provide the employee with immediate personal satisfaction, but the long-run effect again is negative.

When an action plan creates a positive environment, the individual's maximum human needs are at least partially satisfied. His self-image is enhanced. Performance objectives are written, measurable or observable, realistic, specific, and individual. And the result is a positive environment for the win-win situation.

For instance, a manger can encourage an individual's creativity by letting him know that his ideas are appreciated. In the long run, the individual is likely to continue to offer new ideas.

An employee can create a positive environment for his boss by supporting him, or by remaining silent at appropriate moments. This, too, can provide the employee with personal satisfaction; in addition, the long-term relationship remains positive.

The second principle of the OMS, remember, is "Identify and build on strengths." When the action plan satisfies the individual's maximum human need in a positive way, the need can become a strength.

Consider, for example, a manager who has an employee with a maximum human need for economic security. If the manager's action plan helps to satisfy this need in a positive way, the need can be turned into a strength.

A question this manager might ask himself would be "Where can I save money in my organization?" Also: "Would it be a good idea for this person to take on this responsibility?" If the action plan includes placing the employee in a position in which economizing is important, then the need becomes a strength.

Take an employee whose boss has a maximum need to control situations from his own point of view. If the action plan selected by the employee for his boss helps the boss to satisfy his need to control, and does so in a positive way, this need, too, becomes a strength. This employee might ask himself, "How can I let the boss be in control of more situations?" Or: "Would it be possible for me to provide additional opportunities for the boss to control?" If the action plan is based on this approach, then the need becomes an asset.

People feel (and of course they actually are) effective when they can get things done. An action plan helps a person to do this. It also helps point out the difference between real and artificial (or self-imposed) barriers that obstruct action.

In the earlier example of an employee with a maximum need for economic security, a manager might conclude that "I can't put that person in another job." The boss may in fact not be able to relocate that person because of union contracts, company policies, geography, or other reasons. However, he may be able to overcome some of the self-imposed barriers by asking himself "Why not try it?" instead of dwelling on reasons why "it can't be done."

The employee whose boss has a maximum human need to control might say, "I'll try to show him that my way is better," and thus erect a barrier between himself and the boss. Or he might remove the barrier by allowing his boss to be in control.

Remember: An action plan must take into account that human needs are individual and internal. Each person is unique, and the satisfaction of his human needs springs from within. The other person in the relationship only creates the environment in which this need satisfaction can take place.

One might question whether the determination of an individual action plan is manipulative. The answer to this is a definite no. Manipulation is, in effect, forcing another to do what you want him to do regardless of his own desires. In OMS, a person *chooses* to do certain things because they satisfy his own human needs. The action plan seeks to satisfy those needs that already exist within an individual. When an action plan accomplishes a performance objective by satisfying a maximum human need, the individual feels great. So OMS provides the basis for personal satisfaction, especially on the job. In no way can making another person feel great on the job through personal-need satisfaction be termed manipulation.

The action plan is the element of the Open Management System which comes closest to providing the much-sought-after answer card to working with people. The following criteria can serve as guidelines to developing an action plan best suited to satisfy a particular human need.

The appropriate steps to take are listed below for needs identified as minimum, average, or maximum. Keep in mind that the human need around which an action plan should be designed is usually a maximum one.

SELECTION OF THE APPROPRIATE ACTION PLAN

THE NEED FOR ECONOMIC SECURITY

Classifications of Need	*Action Plan Guidelines*
Minimum	Showing this person how he can save money will have little positive effect, since he has a minimum concern for economic factors.
Average	Could be influenced by ways to *save* or *make* more money.

Classifications of Need	*Action Plan Guidelines*
Maximum	Will respond strongly to suggestions on how to *save* or *make* money because of maximum interest in financial matters.

THE NEED TO CONTROL

Minimum	This person will avoid opportunities to take responsibility because of his minimum desire to be in charge.
Average	May be willing to assume some additional responsibilities because of average feelings about the responsibility for decision-making.
Maximum	Will respond well to being put in charge of any activity because of maximum interest in controlling situations in which he is involved.

THE NEED FOR RECOGNITION

Minimum	Prefers to remain in the background because of minimum need for recognition. May respond negatively to being singled out in any way.
Average	Probably will respond positively to situations that call attention to his efforts, because of average desire for attention.
Maximum	Will insist on being in the forefront and will welcome every opportunity to gain additional recognition. Because of a maximum concern for recognition, the need must be reinforced regularly, perhaps several times a day.

THE NEED FOR FEELINGS OF PERSONAL SELF-WORTH

Minimum	Probably will not respond to personal reinforcements of self-worth.
Average	May respond well to positive reassurances

Classifications of Need	*Action Plan Guidelines*
	of personal self-worth because of average feelings about his capabilities.
Maximum	Will respond strongly to regular actions which enhance personal feelings of importance and self-worth.

THE NEED TO BELONG

Minimum	Tends to work most effectively alone, because of a minimum desire to be recognized as a member of the group.
Average	Could respond well to suggestions involving his role within the group, because of an average interest in participating in group activities.
Maximum	Will respond strongly to group acceptance and will resist any efforts that set him apart, because of maximum requirement for participation in the group with which he identifies.

The following examples illustrate practical applications of the action plan.

THE MANAGER'S VIEWPOINT

The Task Force Leader

Ben Wagner, an accountant in the headquarters office, was thirty-two and aggressive, and liked the finer things in life. He was married and had three young children. His home was in a lovely neighborhood, he had two cars, both less than two years old, a boat, and two color TV sets, and he and his family were always stylishly dressed. He was very capable, and his future looked bright.

In addition to his regular job, Ben spent evenings and weekends doing accounting work for other companies. As a result of the late hours on outside jobs, Ben often looked tired during the day.

Ruth Patton, the Accounting Department manager and Ben's boss, was concerned because Ben's effectiveness on the job had diminished. His output had fallen by almost 15 percent. She was aware of his outside accounting work, and knew he did it to earn money for the extra things he wanted. Ruth also recognized that Ben had great potential but that the pace he had set for himself would not help him to get ahead. Ruth wanted to help Ben.

A perceptive manager, Ruth was familiar with the Open Management System. She knew that before she could take any effective action with Ben, she first had to set a performance objective and then identify his maximum human need. So she wrote the following performance objective for Ben:

"To have Ben improve his output by 15 percent within the next sixty days."

A quick review of this objective shows that it was measurable and observable. It was also realistic to expect Ben to accomplish this, and there was a specific time frame of sixty days; Ruth realized that it might take this long for Ben to make the necessary changes in his lifestyle to achieve the goal. The performance objective also was specific, in that it measured output in percentages and within a specific period of time. Finally, it had been written as an individual objective for Ben.

As to the second step, to identify Ben's maximum human need, Ruth had observed the symbols with which Ben surrounded himself. She realized that he, like everyone else, had all five human needs. However, from Ben's human symbols Ruth identified two of these human needs as being in the maximum range: the need for economic security and the need for recognition. As a perceptive manager, Ruth realized that she had to develop an action plan that not only was directed toward the accomplishment of the performance objective but would do this by satisfying Ben's maximum human needs. She decided that of these two needs, the need for economic security was the stronger, and therefore concentrated her efforts toward satisfying this particular need. However, she also kept in mind that Ben had a strong need for recognition as well, and that it was important that the action plan not threaten either need.

Then Ruth was ready for the third step in the Open Management System: developing an action plan. Of course, in considering all the possible actions she could take with Ben, Ruth kept in mind the performance objective that she had set and Ben's maximum human needs.

Finally, Ruth decided on the following plan: She would meet with Ben and offer him an opportunity to be Task Force Leader in a special project. The project was not directly related to his regular work, and required evening and occasional weekend hours, for which Ben would earn extra money. Ruth would also see to it that Ben got recognition for doing this special work. She emphasized to Ben that if he did well as Task Force Leader, his chances for promotion to better-paying jobs within the company would be increased, and he also would gain more recognition. Ruth decided to allow Ben to decide for himself what he would do about his outside accounting work.

The action plan that Ruth decided upon is only one of many possible action plans she might have chosen. Another person might have taken a completely different course of action. However, the main consideration in selecting any plan is whether or not it meets the performance objective and satisfies the maximum human need.

To find out if the plan meets these two vital requirements, follow-up is essential. Ruth scheduled a follow-up for two weeks after putting her plan into action to see if her approach was indeed a good one and decide whether to continue with it or switch to another action plan.

Let's Do It My Way

Mike McCarthy was Production manager of the Jefferson Manufacturing Company. Mike was forty-nine years old, and had come up through the ranks. He was a well-liked, hard-working man with a reputation for standing behind his people. He was also results-oriented, and liked to have things done his way. Mike personally inspected the factory every day and made on-the-spot decisions as soon as he saw something that needed to be done. Although he was tough-minded, he took pride in having his people rise in the organization.

Bill Turner was Personnel manager of the same company. At forty-two, Bill had been with Jefferson Manufacturing for six years. Bill had initiated some innovative personnel programs and personally followed up on them in order to make sure they were being implemented in his way. Bill was smart and aggressive. On one occasion, when one of his subordinates questioned a decision, Bill replied, "We'll do it my way!"

Charles Fletcher was Jefferson's vice-president of Operations. Charles was concerned that with Jefferson's rapid expansion there might soon be a shortage of good young men for responsible future managerial positions. At his last staff meeting, Charles proposed that the Personnel Department accelerate its college-graduate employee-training program to provide for this future need. Bill agreed to cooperate, saying that this was in line with his own thinking. Mike, on the other hand, protested vigorously that the college-trainee program was okay, but what would happen to the many good people he was developing on the line?

Charles realized that his program could become truly effective only with Mike's cooperation. In his approach to resolving the problem, Charles decided to apply the OMS principles. His first step was to write a performance objective for Mike. After reviewing the facts of the situation in his mind, he wrote the following objective:

"To have Mike accept two of the Personnel Department's college trainees for Production Department assignments within ten days."

This objective was measurable, observable, and realistic for Mike at this time, since his department was large enough to accept two trainees within ten days without causing production disruptions. Although Charles wanted Mike to take on more than two trainees in the future, he felt that if he could persuade Mike to accept two at this time, Mike would then see for himself that the program would be advantageous for his department. Further, Charles realized that he had to allow Mike some time to adjust to the situation, and he believed that a ten-day period would be sufficient for this purpose.

The performance objective was specific: It required the acceptance of *two* trainees *within ten days*. It was individual because it was written for Mike.

Charles's second step, of course, was to identify Mike's maximum human need. By observing Mike's words and actions, Charles concluded that his maximum need was the need to control.

Next, Charles had to develop an action plan that would accomplish the objective and satisfy Mike's maximum human needs. He decided to ask Bill to assign two college trainees to the production department. At the same time, he would ask Mike to select two of his most promising employees for rotational assignments in other departments. These rotational assignments would give Mike's people greater exposure within the company and increase their chances for advancement. The details of the rotational assignments for Mike's men were to be handled by the Personnel Department.

Charles, as a perceptive manager, recognized Mike's maximum human need to control, and attempted to satisfy it by creating a situation which he could control in a positive way. Charles also recognized that Bill too had a maximum need to control. So his action plan provided a means by which Bill could also satisfy his need to control in a positive way. Two department managers with the same maximum need were thereby provided with situations in which both could satisfy their needs in a positive way. In addition, Charles was able to implement programs for personnel development which he foresaw as essential to Jefferson in the near future. A win-win situation was created for everyone.

THE EMPLOYEE'S VIEWPOINT

Achiever of the Year

Leroy Peterson was a service engineer for Western Enterprises. For some time he had been trying to persuade Bart Thomas, his boss, to accept a new idea for customer-service contracts. In his efforts, Leroy always emphasized that his idea would lead to more efficient customer services. Bart always listened attentively, but invariably came up with excuses for not accepting Leroy's suggestion.

Leroy had noted in Bart's office numerous pictures of Bart posing with various professional committees. There also was a desk set inscribed by friends on a previous job. On the wall behind his desk Bart had hung a large color photograph of himself receiving the annual Achievement Award from the president of Western Enterprises. Below the picture were the words "Achiever of the Year."

Leroy wanted Bart's approval on his idea for customer service contracts, and decided to apply OMS principles. Leroy's first step was to write a performance objective outlining what he wanted Bart to do. After reviewing the facts, Leroy wrote the following objective:

"To have Bart initiate within two weeks one

customer-service contract which includes my new idea."

Leroy's performance objective for Bart was measurable and observable. It was realistic because it was within Bart's power to initiate a new customer service contract, and specific because the time for the objective to be achieved was stated. It was also individual, because it was written for Bart.

Leroy's second step was to identify Bart's maximum human need. From his observations of Bart's human symbols, Leroy identified Bart's maximum need as the need for recognition.

Finally, Leroy had to develop and implement an action plan that would accomplish the objective and satisfy Bart's maximum human need. Leroy settled on the following plan: He decided to invite Bart to go with him to the customer location he had selected for a tryout of his new idea. Since the customer also favored the idea, Leroy suggested that when Bart arrived he and the office manager would be photographed shaking hands over the new contract.

The action plan that Leroy chose was, of course, one of several that might have accomplished the performance objective. While some people did not care about being photographed, Leroy, a perceptive employee, recognized that Bart probably would respond favorably to the suggestion, because it would contribute to the satisfaction of his maximum human need for recognition.

"Sonny"

Russ Conlon was a sales representative for Dorchester Printing Supply Co. For two years, and with little success, Russ had been trying to increase his share of available business with Greenwood Business Forms, Inc. Dan Newman, Greenwood's aggressive purchasing agent, had been reluctant to give Russ more orders.

Dan seemed to like telling people what to do. He insisted on signing all outgoing mail, and all incoming mail was routed to him first. He enjoyed talking about his long-time relations with salesmen. Dan was fifty-six, and frequently addressed younger salesmen as "Sonny."

Dan ate lunch at the same restaurant every day. He was active in community affairs, and had been overheard to say that he liked to feel he was making a contribution to society. He regularly attended seminars at the local community college, and sometimes took charge of the discussions. He preferred to deal with suppliers who had given him good service in the past.

Russ met often with Dan to try to convince him that Greenwood Business Forms should buy more from Dorchester Printing. Russ had spent a great deal of time emphasizing the quality of his products. He had presented Dan with many descriptive reports and brochures. He had even hinted that for a substantial increase in orders he might get the factory to quote a lower price. Dan seemed interested.

Russ decided to write a performance objective outlining what he wanted Dan to do:

"To have Dan buy 5 percent more Dorchester printing inks than was purchased over the same period last year. This is to be accomplished within four months."

Russ's objective for Dan was measurable and observable. It was realistic because Dan had the authority to place the additional ink orders with Russ. It was specific in that it stated a time at which the objective was to be accomplished. And it was individual because it was written for Dan.

Next, Russ had to identify Dan's maximum human needs. In observing Dan's human symbols, Russ was unable to identify any particular human need as being maximum. He had noted that Dan seemed to have a need to control, a need for economic security, and a need for personal self-worth. At best, Russ felt these three needs were average, and no one need was a maximum.

When there does not seem to be a maximum human need, the one that *appears* to be strongest among the *average* needs is the one that should have first consideration. So even though Russ felt that Dan's need for feelings of personal self-worth was only average, he decided to direct his plan toward the satisfaction of this need.

This brought Russ to step # 3: the development of a plan to help increase his sale of printing inks by 5 percent and satisfy Dan's human need for feelings of personal self-worth. Russ devised an action plan based on the fact that Greenwood was then buying very little ink from Dorchester Printing Supply Co. He decided to suggest to Dan that he use only two of many printing presses for a test. One machine would use Dorchester Type A ink and the second machine would use Dorchester AA ink. After two months, during which time he would consult frequently with Dan, Russ would ask Dan for an evaluation of the two inks and a decision on which best suited his needs.

Russ believed that his plan would contribute to

the satisfaction of Dan's need for feelings of personal self-worth. He also believed that it would help satisfy Dan's need for economic security and his need to control.

Remember that the Module for Working with People includes a section entitled "How Often?" "How Often?" can be a significant factor. If an individual has a need for recognition, it may not be sufficient to provide for its satisfaction once a year, or even once a month. It may require continuous satisfaction. The answer to the question "How often [should a need be satisfied]?" is therefore best answered by the statement "As often as necessary from the other person's point of view."

Obviously, the answer to "How often?" will vary from person to person, and one must always consider the answer in implementing an action plan.

Russ planned to discuss the test inks with Dan on a regular basis—which might have turned out to be once a week or even more often, depending on how Dan responded to the evaluation.

The "In" Group

Walt Edwards was manager of the Claremont branch of the First National Bank. Walt belonged to the local chapter of the Banking Society, the Chamber of Commerce, and a service club. Even though these organizations kept him busy, he obviously enjoyed his memberships. He often spoke of how important it was for the bank to be represented in these organizations.

Terry Burns, one of the loan officers in the Claremont branch, was a young man with excellent growth potential. Terry had been invited to join a new businessmen's group in Claremont. Although it was a small group, it rapidly was achieving a reputation as the "in" group. Everyone at First National was aware that membership in the group usually was not approved for young officers. Terry wanted Walt to approve his membership.

His first step was to write a performance objective, and he decided on the following:

"To have Walt approve within a month my membership for one year in the new businessmen's group."

Terry's performance objective for Walt was measurable and observable. It was realistic because it was within Walt's control to approve the membership. It was specific in that the time in which the approval was to be given was stated. And it was individual because it was written for Walt.

Next, Terry attempted to identify Walt's maximum human need. In watching and listening to Walt, Terry concluded that his maximum need was the need to belong.

Finally, Terry had to develop and implement an action plan that would accomplish his objective and satisfy Walt's maximum need. Keeping in mind Walt's strong need to belong, he decided that Walt probably would welcome the opportunity to participate in a group such as the one Terry had been invited to join. He also recognized that if both he and Walt were members, it would be a splendid opportunity for them to discuss bank problems. So Terry asked the membership chairman of the new businessmen's group to invite both Walt and himself to their next meeting.

Terry believed that after attending, Walt would see that membership in the group would be advantageous to both of them and the bank. At the same time, Walt's need to belong would be satisfied.

14. OMS IN A CHANGING ENVIRONMENT

SO FAR, we have discussed how application of the principles of the Open Management System can help satisfy the needs of people at all levels of business and industry today. The System, in fact, is based on the premise that when one's human needs are satisfied on the job, one's life is more satisfying.

We all have within us the potential to feel good, both on and off the job. But too often, this potential is locked up within us—enclosed by seemingly insurmountable barriers. While it may be true that some of these barriers are imposed by society, we erect most of them ourselves. In effect, we create our own obstacles, which prevent us from satisfying our own human needs. Fortunately, it is also within our power to remove many of these barriers.

Working conditions are changing constantly. People problems have always been a major concern of business. One way to make a start at solving people problems is to be aware of the changes taking place in the work environment. The perceptive observer is one who can distinguish between significant changes and those which only seem to be significant.

At present, people's attitudes toward work are in the process of significant change.

In the early part of this century, people were treated as unique individuals. If the boss liked you, you had a job. If the boss didn't like you, you didn't have a job. During the 1920s the management philosophy of the day was best expressed by Henry Ford, who said, "All you have to do is place the work in front of the men and they will do it." Mr. Ford was a competent manager for his time, and a job at the Ford Motor Company was a highly regarded prize. Paternalism (the "family" concept) was generally accepted.

Beginning in the 1930s, the emphasis shifted from the individual to the group, probably because it was during this period that the labor unions grew to great strength and became a major factor in business. At any rate, the "group approach" seemed to satisfy the human needs of the people in those times.

Today labor unions continue to be strong, and wield great influence in the work environment. However, because the actual work that people do often does not satisfy their human needs, attitudes are changing. Instead of accepting group solutions to human needs, people are expressing a desire for individual attention.

This increased demand for personalized attention to human needs and the trend away from paternalism (the "family" concept) can be found throughout society. It is found in the home, in the relationship between parents and children. Young people today are not willing to accept the traditional reasons for doing things. Children are no longer satisfied and will not accept the parental answer "Because I said so!" to the question of why they should or should not do something.

Similar value changes have revolutionized the military, and the authority of officers over enlisted personnel has been challenged and greatly reduced. Instead of seeing himself as part of his unit, the soldier wants to be treated as an individual.

The church also faces the challenge of changing values. Doctrines that were held inviolable for centuries are questioned, and at the same time the authority of hierarchy is threatened. Here again people are demanding personalized and individual attention to their human needs.

So it is not surprising that the role of management is also being questioned and, as a result, is in a state of change. The role of the employee is changing, too. These changes in the work environment affect all the participants.

We have repeatedly pointed out that individual human symbols tell us a lot about individual human needs. The symbols of a society likewise tell us about needs of that society. It is only necessary to look about to see an endless number of symbols all pointing to the need for individual attention. Styles in dress and hair, office furnishings, coed dormitories, flexible work schedules, the things people talk about—all point to a changing work environment and the need for individual self-determination. Symbols today indicate a general desire to express individuality in all areas of life—including work environment. OMS shows ways to work effectively with others under these changing conditions.

One may or may not like these environmental changes—may or may not be in sympathy with what is taking place in the world of work. We certainly do not suggest that these changes are either good or bad. We do suggest that it is important to be aware of these changes and what they mean to better understand one's role in the changing work environment.

People react to change according to their own point of view. One person accepts or even welcomes certain changes; he may even act to bring about a particular change. This same person may resent other changes and look for ways to avoid participating in them. We all have individual reactions to every change we encounter.

Reacting to a change is not the same as evaulating a change. One cannot help but *react* to change in some way, either positively or negatively. But one can make conscious decisions not to evaluate the change. This concept was expressed succinctly by Dr. Carl Rogers:

"To avoid evaluation or judgment is not to cease having reactions. It may, as a matter of fact, free one to react. 'I don't like what you are doing' is not an evaluation but a reaction. It is subtly, but sharply, different from a judgment which says, 'What you are doing is bad (or good) and this quality is assigned to you from some external source.' "

In OMS, the idea is to focus attention on the problem, not on the symbol of the problem. All too often, people concern themselves with a particular symbol observed in someone else, and then proceed to attack the symbol.

Chronic absenteeism is a symbol of boredom and a paucity of need satisfaction. The only effective approach to the problem is one that treats absenteeism as a symbol indicating that a human need is not being satisfied.

Sometimes restrictions of the work environment do not allow either managers or employees to apply the OMS principles. When this is so, it may very well be that nothing can be done to solve the problem. Examples of such restrictions include the physical layout of a work area, company policies, contractual obligations, a certain production setup. In such circumstances OMS principles are not applicable because of action restrictions, not because of any weakness in OMS.

For instance, there is little opportunity for flexibility on an assembly line, where a certain level of production must be maintained. Where office policy allows for no deviation from established patterns, it may be difficult or impossible to introduce new procedures. Herein lies the challenge to managers and employees—the point, as in all things, is not to complain about what can't be changed, but rather to work creatively around it.

OMS principles create practical approaches to working effectively with people on the job. No involved, theoretical studies are required to apply them. These principles are easy to understand by anyone who wishes to take the time to learn. We all learn constantly—on the job, in the home, in the family, everywhere. OMS consists of logical and practical ways to learn how to create satisfying relationships with others.

Whenever there is a satisfactory relationship with another person, it is because the relationship somehow satisfies that other person's human needs. We all have at least a few satisfying relationships—which is proof that we can learn to have more. One is not always aware of what it is one did to create a good relationship, but through an understanding of the OMS principles the processes involved become increasingly clear.

Some of the Open Management System principles are self-evident. However, OMS correlates them in new ways, and *the result is greater than the application of any one of the princicples alone.* This synergistic relationship makes for a whole which is greater than the sum of its parts. As in bacon and eggs, the combination of elements which are fine in themselves are even better in the combination.

The Open Management System encourages people to become more perceptive and to pay closer attention to what is seen and heard. True, we always see and hear. But how often we fail to understand the underlying meanings!

We also warn against the opposite: It is important not to read more into a situation than is readily apparent. In other words, no amateur psychologizing, please!

In normal work situations, perhaps 90 percent of our relationships tend to be more or less satisfying, or at least neutral, and cause no great problems. But the remaining 10 percent can destroy (or at least adversely influence) the good relationships. While the principles of OMS can, of course, be effectively practiced to improve relationships in the 90-percent area, they can be of greater help in the problem area. The gains in this small but sensitive area will be felt throughout the entire work environment.

To recap briefly, then, the Open Management System deals with the satisfaction of human needs. It is an approach *through which* human needs can be satisfied. It is recognized that in any environment the one most important element contributing to positive feelings is whether or not an individual's human needs are satisfied. This applies everywhere in life, including the home, the job, and one's social world. If what one does contributes to the satisfaction of another's human needs, it will be well received. If it does not contribute to satisfaction or is seen as threatening, it will be resisted. If the activity must be pursued anyway, it will be regarded as dull and boring. It is a tragedy that very often even minor changes can suffice to make a job more satisfying—yet the changes are not made, because the relationship between the job and need satisfaction is not understood.

The Open Management System is also an approach toward motivating people. Motivation is an internal and individual process. One person does not really motivate another. An individual is self-motivating. But it *is* possible for one person to contribute to the environment in which motivation can grow. As a person's human needs are satisfied through OMS, a motivational environment is created, along with opportunities for fulfillment.

The Open Management System is further concerned with maintaining effective lines of communication. Two-way communication. It is a means to opening up and freeing communication from managers toward employees, as well as from employees toward managers.

Through the satisfaction of human needs, the creation of a motivational environment and the breakdown of barriers to communication win-win situations are created, in which manager, employee, and employer all benefit. Actually, the win-win situation as created by the application of Open Management principles extends far beyond the company to include customers, families, friends, and, in fact, the entire society. When people feel good on the job, all of us are the better for it, and tend to handle *all* relationships more fruitfully.

According to a recent report to the Secretary of the Department of Health, Education and Welfare, a definite correlation exists between work and longevity: "In an impressive 15-year study of aging, the strongest predicator of longevity was work satisfaction. The second best predicator was overall 'happiness.' These two social-psychological measures predicated longevity better than a rating by an examining physician of physical functioning, or a measure of the use of tobacco, or genetic inheritance. Controlling these other variables statistically did not alter the dominant role of work satisfaction."

Learning how to work better with people has always been a major concern to managers. Today it is becoming apparent that both managers and employees share in this aim. And in the future this will become even more important. Both the managers and the employees of tomorrow will need to be aware of the necessity of resolving the problems concerning individual human relations. An increase in the skills needed for effectively handling the ever-increasing number of individual human relation situations will most certainly be desirable for all people at work. The Open Management System provides practical, workable ways to develop these skills.